Broken to Beacon

By Robbie Taylor

This book is a memoir written about my Mama through my eyes. This is a true recollection of events. It is not my intention to exaggerate in order to make anyone look good or bad.

www.brokentobeacon.com
ISBN: 978-1543206791

Dedication

For myself
For my family
For my sister
For those other kids like me and my sister
For my Daddy
For my Mawmaw Betty

For my Mama...... "I saw you in the window. I saw you on the street. I saw you in my mirror

looking back at me. I used to pray to not be like you. That was before the sadness fled.

Now I pray to be just like you when it is my turn to be dead."

I would like to thank the following people who helped me in life and aided in the completion of this story: Lynn Griffin, Joye Taylor, Joy Turner, Gail Shields, Denise Greene, Denita Vickers, Patsy Day Salmon, Reverends Debbie and Jackie Potter, Holly Scoggins, Missy Limerick, Liz Freeman, Lisa Rosier, Kathryn Beam, Brenda and Tom Warrick, Joan Robbins, Joanne Jenkins, Lori Toney, Coach Sam Metcalf, Coach Mickey Lineberger, Donna Haynes and family, Susan Metcalf and family, Robby Robertson, Vernon Morrow, Mary Hayes, Jen Delater-Vogelsang, Lisa Bralley, and Cherene Allen-Caraco.

Table of Contents

Advanced Praise

"Hope, acceptance and understanding elude Robbie, her sister Joye, and their Mama throughout numerous hospitalizations, treatments, diagnoses and medications, only to finally find peace in the loving, respectful arms of Hospice when their mother was diagnosed with a terminal medical condition. Why couldn't their mother have been treated with dignity, kindness, compassion and understanding in the mental health system just as she was at the end of her life? "Broken to Beacon" offers a candidly tragic glimpse into a dysfunctional, often ineffective mental health system in need of its own healing and recovery. This book provides insights about how valuing and honoring people can help them overcome extreme emotional distress and leaves its readers to contemplate that, if by taking a page from the "end of life" treatment provided by Hospice, can people labeled with psychiatric diagnoses move beyond the chronicity of an illness-hopelessness cycle to be the whole, complete, strong, and resilient people they truly are". -*Cherene Allen-Caraco, QMHP, QDDP,CESP, CPSS, CEO, Promise Resource Network, Charlotte, NC*

"This is a GREAT read for anyone looking for inspiration! Learn how to forgive the past, accept where you came from and be inspired to live a future with a giving and open heart. This book speaks about realities many of us have lived or have friends, family or loved ones that live through - depression, abusive relationships, lack of self-confidence, mental illness- yet find it hard to discover the courage to ask for help. This book is truly an inspiration and a courageous tale told. True page turner that I could not put down until I reached the end!" -*Jennifer Vogelsang B.A. Psychology, IUSB, Indianapolis*

"This vivid, raw, narrative, which at time assaults the senses, shines, the light on the impact of undiagnosed, misdiagnosed and undertreated mental health issues- on the person, as well as the children, parents and loved ones. It is insightful and engaging, while illustrating the pure, healing power of compassion and love." -*Mary Hays, M.A, LMHC, Indianapolis, IN*

"Taylor pens a raw, gripping account of her mother's painful struggle with mental illness and its devastating impact on her family for years. Yet, through the roller coaster ride of revolving hospital doors-grappling with numerous diagnoses and unsuccessful treatments-peace, light, healing, and unconditional love emerge at her darkest hour. This candid account gives hope to all who fight daily to survive the battle with mental illness and to their families who desperately search for answers."-*Lisa Harris Bralley, M.Ed. retired public high school social studies teacher, current Backpack Food Coordinator of Rutherford County, NC*

Foreword

Imagine for years wishing, hoping, and attempting to die by suicide only to be diagnosed with a terminal illness and "falling in love with life" for the first time. This is the lived experience of Robbie Taylor's "Mama," whose "life was saved by physical death."

"Broken to Beacon" offers a tragic glimpse into the dysfunction, shame, stigma, trauma, domestic violence, and neglect that often accompany a life of mental illness. Written from Taylor's perspective as a child growing up with a mother who experienced 13 suicide attempts, multiple voluntary and involuntary hospitalizations, and a buffet of programs, treatments, diagnoses and medications, all while watching her Mama slowly disappear and become replaced with patient #H707119. That is, until at the age of 64, when Mama re-emerged and the family found peace, tranquility and light after Mama was diagnosed with a terminal medical condition and referred to Hospice. Suddenly, through the loving, respectful arms of the Hospice workers, the hope, restoration, and healing that eluded Robbie, her sister, Joye, and their Mama throughout their lives, was abundant as her Mama was no longer treated like a mental patient, rather was given dignity, grace, freedom, rights and love. The result? "The preyed on became the prayed with, the victim became a victor and the broken became a beacon." Simply put by the author, we are how we treat each other.

As a professional in the mental health community and a person in recovery from emotional distress myself, I contemplate what would have happened if Mama were afforded the same dignity, respect, kindness, compassion, and quality treatment within the mental health system as she was at the end of her life. If supports designed around recovery, restoration and healing were available at the time of her last hospitalization rather than the same recommended outpatient and inpatient options as the previous 30 plus years, would the family have mended and would Mama have been able to enjoy the serenity and peace in life as she did near death?

"Broken to Beacon" offers a candidly tragic glimpse into a dysfunctional, often ineffective mental health system in need of its own healing and recovery. This book provides insights about how valuing and honoring people can help them overcome extreme emotional distress and leaves its readers to contemplate that, if by taking a page from the "end of life" treatment provided by Hospice, can people labeled with psychiatric diagnoses move beyond the chronicity of an illness-hopeless cycle to be the whole, complete, strong, and resilient people they truly are. *-Cherene Allen-Caraco, QMHP, CESP, QDDP, CPSS CEO and Founder, Promise Resource Network Charlotte, NC*

Section 1: Dark Corner

Chapter 1- Babies Having Babies

My Mama, Barbara Jean Morrow was born at home on Saturday, May 28, 1949 around lunch time. She weighed just over six pounds and was delivered by Dr. Lovelace. He delivered most all the babies and was the primary caregiver for folks in the county back then. Mama and her parents (Betty Jean Honeycutt and Harold Watson Morrow), lived in the Dark Corner Community in Rutherford County, North Carolina, with her paternal grandparents (Granny Anniebelle and Papa Otis). They lived not too far from the old narrow steel Big Island bridge. It ran over the mighty Broad River where some of our family members were baptized. The community church where they attended was just down the road a piece and was called Broad River Baptist Church. Some were married there and some were buried there.

It was an oppressed little area in the foothills of the Great Smoky Mountains where money ran thin and back breaking labor was the only way of life. Those old mountains were the perfect backdrop for them daylight to dawn hard working people. The roads were all dirt and there were outhouses at every homeplace. Most people were sharecroppers, farmers, or cotton pickers. Horses and mules were still being used in the fields to plow and till the earth. Mama's parents were blue collar workers but prior to that picked cotton and farmed even when they were children. In fact, Mama's Mama started picking cotton when she was only five years old in order to help her family make ends meet. When she was eight years old she finally started getting paid.

Mama's parent's money was tight but they had more than a lot of people in their community at that time. They doted on Mama but they were also a bit strict. Her home life was filled with love and she got all of what she needed and most of what she wanted. Eventually in 1962 they had saved up enough money to buy their own place. It was just down the road a few miles in the Holly Springs Community. It was a 30 year old small country home with just shy of two acres. It sat on a hill and they put in running water and a bathroom. No more outhouses! Pawpaw still went outside to the woods every night to go to the bathroom. Guess you can take the boy outta the country but you can't take the country outta the boy! Thus, the homeplace on the hill had been established for Mama and her family.

Mama was often nagged at to get out of bed and get ready for school. She wasn't very motivated even as a young child. That often caused friction between her and her mama (my Mawmaw Betty). Nevertheless Mawmaw's love for Mama was undeniable and had no limits. She was always there for her no matter what. When Mama would mess up she would get an ear full from Mawmaw but her love for Mama was unconditional. It didn't matter if she was right, wrong, up or down. Mawmaw lost friends and family because of her loyalty to Mama. They were the greatest of friends and each other's nemesis. Their relationship was sometimes volatile, disappointing, codependent, doting, toxic, enabling, brilliant, and awesome. They were a beautiful mess!

Mama had quite a few friends and she was somewhat popular as a young girl. Mawmaw and Pawpaw's homeplace on the hill was always open to her friends. Her paper dolls were the envy of her first friend that also happened to be her Aunt Joy Honeycutt (Mawmaw Betty's baby sister). They were the same age except Aunt Joy was 4 months older than Mama. She was an only child but she and Aunt Joy were as close as sisters. Aunt Joy said Mama always had lots of candy and nice dresses. Mawmaw made all of her clothes and she kept up with the styles of the times. She was a superior seamstress and Mama quickly followed in her footsteps and learned to sew.

Mama's best friend in school was Patsy Day. On her 10th birthday, at their old house in Dark Corner, Mawmaw gave Mama a party. It was kind of a big deal since most people couldn't afford to give their children parties. In fact, Patsy had never been to a birthday party before. She was excited to go and give her best friend a gift. She had picked out a rubber ball for Mama so they could play kickball together. According to Patsy, "they had loads of fun" that day.

When Mama and Patsy got to high school they became "bestest" friends. They were inseparable. They would write each other ten page letters even though they saw each other every day. They had to catch the school bus and ride it to Harris Elementary School, then change buses to go on to Chase High School. However, they didn't always go on to the high school. They would sometimes skip class and walk back to the homeplace on the hill. They would hang out there all day and then clean up so there would be no evidence when Mawmaw came home from her seamstress job. They would have gotten an ear full from Mawmaw if she would have known. Patsy would often spend the night with Mama but Mawmaw would never let Mama go to Patsy's simply because she had a brother. Mawmaw thought that would not be proper.

Eventually Patsy became my "Aunt Patsy" and my Godmother. Aunt Patsy told me she and Mama were always good girls. They never got into any trouble. They didn't drink or touch drugs. She would smoke cigarettes once in awhile but Mama was never a smoker. She also told me she used to be the look out while Mama and Daddy made out. She said she was probably in the same room when I was conceived. TMI Aunt Patsy TMI. Daddy came home on military leave and that's when it happened.

Mama got pregnant with me in January of 1966. She and Daddy, Robert (Dinky) Norris Taylor quickly got married on February 8, 1966. She was only sixteen years old and my Daddy was nineteen. Mama told me they got pregnant on purpose so Mawmaw would allow them to marry. Mama's daddy, Pawpaw Harold never knew she was pregnant before she got married. He thought I was premature. That turned out to be a well- kept secret.

Mama eventually dropped out of high school while pregnant with me. She told me it was because the other girls at school were talking about her but Aunt Joy told me it was probably Mama's way of not having to go to school since she hated it anyway.

Mama and Daddy were madly in love. Daddy was in the Army and he would go AWOL just to come home and see Mama and me. He was always doing wild things like that. I don't know if he was reckless, crazy, or convicted to do things his way no matter what. He liked to raise a little cain and do whatever he wanted to. I reckon' he thought the rules of life didn't apply to him. He did things the "Dinky" way.

Daddy was a slender and handsome young man. He was about 5'8" and weighed 125 lbs. soaking wet. He was an exceptional athlete and excelled at any sport he tried. He could steal a ball, steal a base, or run for a touchdown in nothing flat! He had a work ethic in all aspects of his life that was undeniable. His Taylor blue eyes were striking. Mama fell head over heels for my handsome Daddy. He told me he and Mama used to play in mud puddles together when they were little. He knew her all of his life. Their love was a not always pretty bond but it remained between them eternally.

I was born in September of 1966. They named me after my Daddy. He wanted a boy and planned to name his newborn son Robert after himself. Instead he got me and they named me Roberta Gail. The name Gail is Mawmaw's sister's name. I was called Robbie from the day I was born. I had my Mama's green eyes and Daddy's laid back temperament.

My parents doted on me but my Mawmaw Betty was my first love. She took over my care early and often. Sometimes it was out of necessity, sometimes it was out of lack of confidence in Mama's parenting skills, and sometimes it was out of pure love for me.

They lived with Mama's folks and Mawmaw tried to keep Daddy in line too. That was a tough job. He was a good guy and loved his family but he was immature and didn't have "good raisin" according to Mawmaw. Once he was talking hateful to Mama and Mawmaw whipped him with a washing machine hose. She didn't put up with his shenanigans.

In November of 1968 when I was just over two years old, Mama ran off and left me with Mawmaw. She was worried sick because she didn't know where Mama had gone. That was my first taste of abandonment, Mama choosing a man over me, and Mawmaw rescuing me. Rumor had it she had run off with one of the Allen boys. She disappeared. Poof. Gone. I guess the pressure of being a teen mother and young bride was too much for her. She eventually turned up at Aunt Gail and her husband Glen's house in South Carolina. She stayed there about three weeks. That was the first of many times Mawmaw came to my rescue.

Mama finally came home and she and Daddy reconciled. Not too long after that Mama was pregnant again. A miscarriage followed. Mama received no counseling and talked very little about her miscarriage. I asked her about it once and she told me she started bleeding and lost the baby quickly. She didn't elaborate and I didn't push her.

Eventually my parents moved out of the homeplace on the hill and rented a small house in Forest City, NC. Aunt Patsy said it was right behind Florence Baptist Church on Beaver Street. Even back then one of Mama's challenges was keeping the house clean. There was a little something that was off because Mama grew up in a neat, clean, and tidy home. Aunt Patsy told me of a time when she went there to visit and all the dishes in the house were dirty. She said Mama did take good care of me though and I was always clean when I was a baby. Aunt Patsy encouraged Mama and tried to help her. Mama was about 19 years old at that time.

Shortly after that Aunt Patsy got married. Mama went with them to the courthouse. When Aunt Patsy said "I do", Mama was holding her hand behind her back and she whispered in her ear, "I do too". She and her new husband Rex didn't have much money and Christmas was coming. Mama gave Aunt Patsy some of her own Christmas ornaments so her tree would look pretty. There was one particular ornament that she gave her that was special. It was a small glass strawberry shaped ornament that probably cost 10 cents. That ornament would become important in their relationship over the years. She was always generous and passionate about giving. She loved Aunt Patsy with her whole heart and sharing with her was natural.

My sister came along in January of 1970. They almost named her Caroline after the Neil Diamond song. Instead, they named her Joye after Mawmaw's baby sister Joy also known as Mama's aunt. Joye's middle name was Elaine after a family friend. We lovingly referred to my baby sister as Little Joye and Mama's baby girl. She was the apple of our parent's eyes. She got Daddy's striking Taylor blue eyes. Our parents loved them some baby girl and spoiled her rotten. Mama wrote in my baby book that I asked her where they got Joye. She replied, "God gives us babies because he thinks we deserve them."

Chapter 2 The Light Brown Skates

Mama was having health problems and had to have a complete hysterectomy in 1971 when she was 22 years old. I was in first grade and a classmate asked me why my Mama was in the hospital. I told her so she wouldn't have any more babies. My teacher told Mama what I had said and it made her laugh. To my knowledge she never had any hormone therapy. Looking back I feel confident not having hormone replacement therapy aided in her future issues.

Mama and Daddy bought a brand new mobile home and had it put on a lot at Morning Star Trailer Park in Danieltown, NC. Daddy's brother Lester (also lovingly known by my Daddy as simply "Brother") and his wife and kids lived right beside us. We were a close knit family. Our cousins Diane, Marie, and Leslie were about our age and we spent a lot of time with them. Unfortunately Joye and I never knew the rest of Daddy's family very well including his parents.

When I was 6 years old and in the first grade, an eighth grade girl was bullying me on the bus. I was small for my age and younger than the other kids because my birthday was in late September. That bully was relentless. I told Mama about it and she pitched a fit! My 22 year old Mama was waiting for the bus that afternoon when it dropped me off. She got on the bus and had a few words with whoever was listening and I never got bullied again. I didn't hear what she said but I do know she liked to cuss a lot and I bet those kids on the bus heard words they had never heard before! I think Mama would have killed someone without batting an eye when it came to me and Joye.

We had a good life there. It was as normal as a young cotton mill family could be in the early 70's in Rutherford County. Many people dropped out of high school to go to work in the thriving local cotton mills. The next natural step was to get married and have kids. That was the norm for the area and the era. The money was decent and it afforded families to buy their own home. Daddy was a hard worker and a good provider. Mama said he played way too much golf though.

Mama's paternal grandmother (Granny) stayed with us often. She helped get us ready for school and took care of us. I remembered my school bus number because it was the same number as my Granny's age, 67. Her name was Anniebelle Morrow. She was born in 1904 and she always wore dresses. She was thrifty, loving, kind, and worked very hard in the fields most of her life. She had a little two room tiny house beside the homeplace on the hill. It didn't have a bathroom so the outhouse was where she and anyone that visited her did their business. When me and Joye spent the night with her we used an empty Crisco can as our temporary toilet.

Her home also had an active honeybee hive attached to the outside of it. She had the hive harvested each year by a bee keeper and would share the sweet bounty with her community. Once I was staying with her and I saw her grab her pistol and shoot a squirrel out of the tree 15 feet from her front door. She proceeded to prepare it. She said she had a hankering for squirrel for supper. She dipped Tube Rose snuff and was the best spitter I ever knew. She was on a meager fixed income yet never failed to have every person in her family something for Christmas and birthdays. She was a great example of living generously and giving even if you have little.

She read her Bible every night of her life. She kept up with marriages, births, and death dates and wrote them in the blank pages in her Bible. Somehow I ended up with her Bible and it is one of my most precious possessions. Granny was always good to me and Joye. Mama loved Granny and turned to her for help over the years.

Mama liked to do hair so she went to cosmetology school. Joye and I had the most interesting hair colors during that time. Mama would experiment on us. Joye's hair was naturally blonde but mine was sandy colored. In one of our old pictures our hair was platinum blonde! Mama would also tie my hair up in little curls by using socks. That made my hair curlier. Sometimes she would braid it while it was still wet so the curls were tighter. Joye's hair was thick, pretty, and styled easily. Mama was always styling, cutting, or dying our hair.

Mama was a very attentive and loving mother. She was sweet to us when we got sick or didn't feel good. She would lay down with us and snuggle. Sometimes we would curl up behind her knees when she was napping on the couch. She was always affectionate and kissed and hugged us often. Gimme some sugar (give me kisses) and I love you's were a common exchange between Mama and her girls. There was no doubt that she loved us and we were her heart.

She kept our baby books up to date and she doted on us. To say she was a proud Mama was an understatement. She was a grade mom when I was in first grade. That was a mom who went to school and took snacks, read to the children, and was present in the classroom. My first understanding of compassion happened during that time. A little girl in my class always came to school dirty. She also had lice in her hair. She was from a poor family and one that obviously needed a hand. I had the privilege of witnessing my Mama wash the little girl's hair in the tiny sink in our classroom. I watched her take some of my clothes to school and change my classmate's clothes in the morning and change them back in the afternoon. Even at 6 years old I knew Mama was doing something extra special. I could feel the compassion in her heart in my heart.

On the completion of my first grade year I was asked if I wanted the classroom pet. It was a gerbil named Irvin. Mama welcomed Irvin into our family. Unfortunately Irvin quickly went to heaven so Mama got me Irvin #2 because I was sad. She loved animals and she loved me so getting another gerbil was a no brainer. She also got me a dog and we named him Tag after Santa Claus's dog. She spoiled me a lot.

She kept me and Joye active. We tried lots of different things. We both were in Brownies and Girl Scouts. She also enrolled me in baton and Joye and I were both in parades. Mama taught me how to roller skate when I was 2 years old. She would take me with her to the Danieltown skating rink. That was the beginning of a childhood filled with a love for skating rinks. We made friends there that would turn out to be as close as family.

That was where Mama and me met our lifelong friend Gina Tate. Gina had light brown skates that the skating rink owner bought just for her to wear! It was unusual for a girl to have skates that were not white. Mama thought they were cool and therefore so did I. She never pointed out that Gina's light brown skates were different. Mama always embraced people's uniqueness including my own. Everyone was allowed to dance to the beat of their own drum not with just tolerance but with acceptance and encouragement.

On any given Friday and Saturday night Joye and me could be found with a group of kids at a skating rink somewhere in our county. I can still hear Freddy Fender belting out "Wasted Days and Wasted Nights." That was the first time I ever heard Spanish words. "The Locomotion" was also a funky song they played while we skated and did the limbo. Mama knew we loved it and it was cheap fun. She would drop us off at 6:00 PM and pick us up at 10:00 PM. She felt comfortable dropping us off unsupervised because back then there was very little crime. Me and that little rascal sister of mine were skating fools! We would also have a little change in our pocket for candy or a snack.

When I was 8 and Mama was 24, she had a brand new, bright red Chevy Malibu that Pawpaw helped her buy. It was so cool! Mama was hot stuff in my book. Once I was with her and we got pulled over for speeding in that Malibu. Unfortunately she had a bit of a lead foot. We were doing over 90 miles an hour on old highway 74 halfway between the Tri City Mall and Spindale. She eventually wrecked and totaled her Malibu in the curve on Sulpher Springs Road. That was scary but Mama was still cool.

Joye and me had bikes, skateboards, and Big Wheels. We played with dolls, shot basketball, hit baseballs and softballs. We made our bases out of cow patties in the pasture. We both were in the school band. I played the drums and Joye played the trumpet. I don't know how Mama afforded it but we wanted to try band and somehow she figured out how to pay for it. Daddy helped with that a little but it was a hardship on them both.

We played in the creek and climbed trees. We built our own tree house (ok Joye mostly built the treehouse) and used moss as the carpet for our homemade forts. Mama gave us the freedom to play rough, be tomboys, and bought us dolls when we asked for them. Joye liked Baby Tender Loves and I loved my Ms. Beasley doll. We played outside until the sun went down. Mama just let us be who we were. Both of us loved rasslin' (wrestling) and football. For Christmas one year Mamasanta brought us cool NFL Los Angeles Rams football jackets. They looked like Chase High letter jackets because the Rams and the Trojans of Chase High were the same colors. We thought we were somethin'.

My sister and I had lots of friends growing up. Some were from school and some were from other activities such as softball, baseball, and any of the other things Mama had us busy doing. Many of those friends we had since we were very young. Our friends loved Mama and she loved them. She related to young people and genuinely cared for each and every one of them. She was outgoing, young, and very involved with me and Joye. She was fun loving and easy to talk to. She just had a way of making those around her feel important and cared for.

Chapter 3- The Separation

Daddy had a cool orange Gran Torino. He liked cars and racing them. Unfortunately he liked women and booze a lot too. He and Mama separated a few times over the years and eventually divorced in 1974 when I was 8 and Joye was 5. Mama got full custody of us and Daddy was supposed to get us every other weekend. He was good about paying child support and we visited him once in awhile. There was always some type of drama surrounding our visits with Daddy though. Loud voices were used more often and the energy in the air was more tense. According to the child custody agreement, Daddy was not supposed to take us out of the state of North Carolina. He was not very interested in rules so he took us to Myrtle Beach which is in South Carolina. He didn't tell Mama and Mawmaw that he was doing that and it caused them significant worry. He would never hurt us but he liked to do things his way even if it scared others.

After the separation Joye and me heard a lot over the years about how our Daddy, his mama, and his daddy were not exactly fit to help raise us. Daddy and his daddy (Pawpaw Pete) used to drink together often and a lot. They once brought a watermelon over to our house and left it on the steps for us. Mama wouldn't let us eat it because she didn't trust them when they were drinking. Joye and me didn't really know Daddy very well back then. He would never hurt us. We were his world. That was a tough time for him. He was losing his family and he was still a young man trying to find his way. At times he would do stupid things to get Mama's attention. Daddy respected (or was scared of) Mawmaw and he knew she would do whatever it took to protect her girls. Mawmaw didn't play when it came to her girls and Daddy knew that. Mawmaw had put a whuppin' on him before and he knew she would do it again.

Shortly after our parents divorced, Mama's daddy died suddenly from a massive heart attack in 1975 at our homeplace on the hill. Me and Joye were there with Mawmaw when it happened but Mama was a challenge to locate because she was off with one of the Allen boys again. Losing Pawpaw was devastating for Mama and Mawmaw. Watching the two of them grieve was painful. He worked hard and loved his family. He was Mama's rock and she relied on him.

Mawmaw received a year's salary from pawpaw's death. She used some of that money to pay off some bad checks Mama had written. Mawmaw always had Mama's back and enabled her. Also, their house was immediately paid off due to an insurance policy they had taken out to protect each other. What a wise decision that was to keep Mawmaw from having to worry about a house payment ever again.

After the divorce Daddy began dating. They soon moved in together. We could visit Daddy anytime he wanted as long as Mama didn't have any plans with us. There was the court ordered weekend visitation with Daddy but that didn't matter to our parents. When we were old enough to call home, Mama didn't mind if he wanted to spend extra time with us any weekend. They had started being more cordial and agreeable when it came to me and Joye. Thank goodness. Most of our visits to his home were fine. He was usually drinking but we still enjoyed our time with him. He would take us fishing. Daddy and Joye would catch all kinds of fish. I enjoyed it but they ruled in the fish catching. He took us bowling or to play some kind of ball. As we got older he added playing pool to our agenda. We were tomboys, reckless barefoot creek loving tree climbing, and baby doll toting girls. Daddy got two daughters that loved most things he did but he loved us as just his girls too.

Mama remarried in 1976. He was a good guy. He was kind to us and Mama seemed to care deeply for him but he drank a lot. Once I found a letter that Mama had written to him. In the letter it said that she loved him more than anything in the world. It hurt my feelings because I wanted her to love me and Joye more than anything in the world. She explained it to me and soothed me. She was sweet about the letter and didn't mean to hurt my feelings.

Our stepdad engaged with us and played sports with us some. He taught me and Joye how to throw a spiral football. He told us stories about his Army adventures in Greece. He was a cook and it sounded exotic and interesting. He really was a decent guy.

Eventually that marriage dissolved but Mama kept his last name. They were together 4 years but were legally married 12 years. Later on when I grew up, Daddy told me he used to hate our stepdad because he took his family from him. I told Daddy our stepdad was kind to us and that he was a very good guy. That seemed to be a relief for Daddy. He worried about us obsessively. He knew in his heart he had let us down and it ate him up.

Chapter 4- Mama the Example

Mama was my first coach. Our eight year old Harris-Shiloh Little League girls' softball team name was the Squaws. Mama picked it out. It was not a politically correct name back then but it was simply a very cool team name that no one else had. Joye was our team mascot. She was always involved with whatever was going on and she was stuck to Mama's side like velcro kid. She also coached our softball team the next year and she decided that we would be called the Angels. We went from Indian girls to heavenly spirits in one year! We played softball at Harris Elementary School. That was where Joye and I went from kindergarten through eighth grade. Mama was also our cheerleading sponsor over the next several years. We cheered the Mighty Mites and Pee Wee's football teams at Chase High School. Mama designed and made most of our blue and gold uniforms. She came up with the idea to have our names monogrammed on our cheerleading bloomers. She put her girls first above everything and she wanted us to have the very best.

Mama's heart was huge to a fault and she set a precedent for me and Joye. She was always helping strays or wounded animals. I recall a time when one of our chickens pecked one of our kitten's belly and caused its intestine to poke through its skin. Mama took a needle and thread, pushed the kitty's intestines back inside its belly and sewed it up by hand. That kitty turned out to be just fine. Going to the vet wasn't an option financially so she just did what she had to do. In fact, none of our animals had ever been to a vet nor did I even know where a vet was! Mama got her love of animals from Granny Morrow and me and Joye got it from Mama.

For a few years girls softball was suspended, but that didn't stop the Taylor girls. Mama signed us up for Minor League and Little League baseball. We played with the boys and were readily accepted. Joye and me held our own when it came to any sport with any girls or boys. Mama and Daddy both were athletic and so were we. Give us a ball of any kind and we were happy.

She would also pick up different kids in our community and take them to whatever practice was in season. We would load up in her old baby blue station wagon. Gas money was always low but it was important to Mama to get us and anyone else that needed a ride to practice and games on time.

Chapter 5- Mama is Cool

We had fantastic birthday parties when we were little. Lots of our cousins, kids in the community, and their parents would come and visit. There was cake with candles, gifts, and food. Mawmaw always made our cakes and Mama usually organized the parties. Christmas was festive too. We decorated the house and the tree. Mama was quite talented and crafty. She knew how to knit, cross stitch, and sew. She was pretty dang good at making things and generally being creative. She enjoyed making homemade bows for our presents and they always looked professionally wrapped. She liked to put a little extra touch on the things she did for us.

Mama was super hip and she dug music. She constantly had some type of music playing. Usually it was 70's rock on the eight track player. She helped instill in me a love of music that was like a fire burning. On January 5, 1978 she took me to see the rock band KISS. I was 12 years old and she was 28. The tickets were $8.00 each. I wasn't sure how she afforded to buy them for me but I was grateful. It was their ALIVE II tour. I remember the excitement and the thrill of watching the show. That was the first time I smelled marijuana. We rode the hour long drive to the old Charlotte Coliseum on Independence Boulevard in Charlotte, NC. My lifelong obsession with music was ignited by that experience. It was too freaking cool and an unforgettable adventure. Who does that? Mama was a cool chick in my book!

In 1979 Mama took me to see the movie "The Rose" starring Bette Midler. I was 13 and looking back now that movie was a bit mature for me but I loved it! The music was fantastic and the storyline about a living hard rock and roll chick was right up my young hearts alley! I was grateful to get to see it and I bought the soundtrack just as soon as I could. I knew every word to every song on that 8 track tape and still do.

In the late 70's a country music band hooked Mama. They played at a bar in Myrtle Beach, SC, which happened to be Mama's favorite place on the planet. She watched them play over and over. She got to know each of them. She had a special relationship with one of the guys. They dated, were friends, and were pretty close. I remember when their songs first started playing on the radio, Mama would squeal with delight and pride. She loved them. When the band started touring, one of the guys wrote her and asked her to come to their concert at the University of Tennessee in Knoxville. Mama was financially unable to go and that was the last time she ever had contact with him. Years later during Mama's illness, I tried to contact them to let them know she was sick and see if they could call, write, or visit. I never heard back from them unfortunately. If only she had went to that Knoxville concert who knows what would have happened.

Mama always took us to the beach at least once a year. We could never afford to go but that didn't matter. Sometimes a shoebox full of change was all that was between us and another night's stay. Mama never failed to figure it out. It was always Myrtle Beach she took us to. That was the only beach Joye and me ever knew existed. When the word beach was referenced, we assumed Myrtle Beach was being spoken about and still do.

Section 2- The Locusts Start to Eat

apter 6- Move On

ie beach (Myrtle Beach). I was 12 years old. We were
r Bridge on Hwy 501 in Florence, SC. Her old red Vega
18-wheeler stopped to help us. Mama climbed into the
by the window on the passenger side. I remember how
tranger and me. I knew even then she had intentionally
was a calming feeling to an already anxious little girl.
. He dropped us off and Mama thanked him. He said he
and children. That experience stuck with me. I drive
ways think of Mama, the truck driver, and me. That old
know how we got back home either. That car was
nd we never saw any of it again. It didn't seem to be too

Chapter 7- Committed Consistency

After Mama's second marriage dissolved in 1978, when she was 29, things began to change. Our house got messier, she started to see different men, and her anger seemed to come out of nowhere. It was as if a light switch had a dimmer on it and it was slowly but surely turning dark. She was a single mother of two little girls and trying to raise us on minimum wage was taking its toll on our family. She was a seamstress and struggled to keep it together financially and emotionally. She wanted us to have things like the other kids and did her best to make that happen. However, things at home were challenging for my sister and me. We didn't see Daddy very often and Mama needed help. Mawmaw did the best she could to help us. She made sure we had the things we needed and she was there for us.

Mama's new rage and consistent digression was not a normal riff between mothers and daughters. It was a desperate woman not realizing that a dark passenger had climbed into her life. Our lives. She started to refer to me as lazy and the reason her life was a mess. She began to tell me she hated me over and over and I started to believe her. She began smacking me around and once I had to stay out of school because of that. Her left hand was powerful. It was full of love and full of pain. It used to soothe us and hold us but it had changed.

We moved from trailer park to trailer park pretty often but we never left the county. We lived in a tiny trailer on Harrilltown Hill and then we moved into a bigger one about two doors down. We also lived at Clayton's trailer park in Sandy Mush and we lived in some apartments in Spindale over by Duke Power. We were running from the rent bill but no matter where we moved Mama made sure we never had to change schools. That was one of the few consistencies we had. It was very important to her even though the world around her was getting darker and darker and changing fast. She did everything she could to keep us in the same school and continue our extracurricular activities. When I was in the seventh grade and Joye was in the third grade I had basketball practice at 7:30 each morning. Mama would drop us off at Jim Cole's store on Highway 221 every morning before she went to work. She had made arrangements with handsome Jim and his sweet wife Linda to let us wait there.

The Cole's were always good to our family. Mama had made an additional arrangement with one of the teachers (who was also my basketball coach at school) to stop by and pick us up every morning at Jim Cole's store. Mr. Robbie Robertson picked us up in his little red Datsun truck day after day. So there we were. Mr. Robertson, Joye, and me riding down Highway 221 with some '70's rock music blasting on the radio. He helped hone my early love for music and my basketball skills. He was one of many people that went the extra mile to help our little family. Mama's determination to keep us at the same school was admirable and successful. We both went to Harris Elementary and we never had to change schools even through the madness Unfortunately though, the locusts had started to eat and we (not just Mama) were becoming broken.

Chapter 8 - Squalor

Our old trailer from Morning Star Lake Trailer Park had been moved behind Mawmaw's homeplace on the hill. We moved back into it and soon it was littered, disheveled, and filthy. We swept all the trash out the back door over the years. We swept papers, boxes, trash, animal shit, or whatever else we could get the broom on literally out the back door. There was a mound of garbage that had accumulated underneath the back door. There were no steps so everything fell on the ground. I felt anxious about it but didn't know why because that was our normal. My bedroom was on the opposite end of the house and it had a tiny bathroom in it. I don't recall ever using that bathroom because it had clothes and trash piled up to the ceiling. My room was always exceptionally disheveled. I remember the stress that I felt because of it. Why didn't I just clean it up? It was an unexplained and undiagnosed anxiety. Joye's room was also a mess. She couldn't go in it or sleep in it. It was used for storage and was a catch all. There were clothes, toys, coat hangers, and junk piled up to the ceiling.

Joye and I slept in sleeping bags or pallets (southern term for blankets) on the floor. We would sleep in the living room a lot. We always had dogs and cats in the house and they would sleep in our sleeping bags with us. We would argue pretty much every day about whose turn it was to clean up shit from the animals. Our nasty home emulated the nastiness Mama felt inside. She was feeling ugly on the inside so the outside became ugly too.

The electricity was cut off from time to time and food ran thin. In the winter, the fuel oil we used for heating was often a challenge to get. She couldn't afford it. But when the electricity was on we used the oven to warm us sometimes. Mama was holding on but the stress was overpowering her. She could barely feed us. In fact, a few times our church stepped in and brought us groceries and clothes. I'm not sure how they knew but I was and am grateful. Once I went out to our Uncle Vernon's trailer next door. I snuck in and "borrowed" a can of corn. He would have given us the corn if I would have asked. Maybe I didn't want him to know. Uncle Vernon was one of the best men I ever knew. He taught me how to play poker when I was 9, ride with him on his tractor, and how to give back to our community by being an example of generosity. He also taught me that anyone can adapt and overcome if they set their mind to it. He had been in a wheelchair most of his adult life. He lived independently, relied on no one, and helped anyone in need.

Chapter 9- Abandonment

Mama grew more ill-tempered and hateful each day. Me and Joye caught the wrath of her struggles quite often. She couldn't or didn't hide the fact that we were a burden at times. A burden she loved but a burden nonetheless. She had started saying things I thought she really meant. She would tell us to go to hell or she wished we were never born or I was the reason for her fucked up life. She made sure and let us know that we would come home from school one day and she would be gone. Which day would be the day? I was sick to my stomach all of the time because of the impending doom of abandonment. It was real. She said so.

Once she took us to her paternal grandmother's (Granny's) house in Fingerville, SC. Granny moved there in 1978. I was probably 11 and Joye was about 7. It was in the summer and we were going to stay a few days or so I thought. She didn't come back and we didn't hear from her. I assumed we were going to live with Granny. I was trying to figure out how I was going to take care of my sister and how we would be able to go to school. We were there for a few weeks until she finally came back and got us. I really thought maybe she was done with us.

A year or so later Mama and I were at Kmart and I lost sight of her. I couldn't find her. I started to cry because I thought she had left me there. I was too old to be crying but I was afraid. Anxiety took over my little body like bad butterflies, bees, and adrenaline. That was part of the beginning of an undiagnosed anxiety disorder that would chase me throughout my life and attempt to cripple me. It was a deep dark secret I carried around with me like a thousand pound boulder. A weight that caused me to break out into hives and have full blown panic attacks. I never told a soul. I was afraid and ashamed. I was 12.

Chapter 10- I Hate You

One evening Mama had a male visitor. I woke up in the night, looked out the window, and his truck was still there. He was in bed with Mama and I was enraged. My sister was in her sleeping bag on the floor in Mama's room. I ran from the room screaming that I hated her. I don't know what happened but I know what it looked like to my childish eyes. I crawled in my sleeping bag on the living room floor and covered my head while I chanted I hate you over and over. She came to console me and she said it wasn't what it looked like. I instinctively knew that whatever had taken place had been inappropriate. I knew it in my bones and in my soul. That man (one of the Allen boys again) had no business in our home and Mama should have known better. Did she know better? What was wrong with her? It made my guts hurt. It was awkward, humiliating, and embarrassing. What about my sister? What was she doing in there? What did she hear or see? It was too much pain to process at that age.

Born to Lose 2/15/95

From the womb
To the world
Cast into hate and pain
Dancing around lightning
Crawling in the rain
Shadows of doubt
And I am to blame
Enfolding me in chaos
And engulfing me in shame
From the cradle to the grave
I was never free to choose
I was born to lose……

Plant weeds and weeds will grow.

Chapter 11- The Ass Magnet Round One

Mama had become an ass magnet. Our lives as we knew it no longer existed. The good stuff was in the rear view mirror. She continued to evolve for the worse and was nose diving rapidly. Whatever was happening to Mama was happening to our little family, not just her. She met a young guy that was 19 years old. She was 29. That was a big deal since I was 13 and he was only a few years older than me. It was not a popular relationship to say the least. That was Mama's first physically abusive relationship that I knew of.

In 1978, Mawmaw remarried and moved to Rock Hill, SC, which was almost two hours away. We still lived in the mobile home behind Mawmaw's homeplace on the hill. Mama's new boyfriend moved in with us. I don't remember him ever having a job. Mama continued to struggle to make ends meet. She had an old blue Ford station wagon that she constantly had trouble with, two little girls that needed clothes, and food that needed to be put on our table. No matter how hard things got she would bring me and Joye McDonald's food for supper every Thursday on pay day and we loved it. It was a special treat that we relished and looked forward to. It was a glimpse of light in our new darkness.

I started staying away from home often. I thought that would make Mama happier since apparently she hated me and never seemed to care where I was anyway. I began to spend a lot of time with a family from church, Brenda and Tom Warrick. I played church softball for them. They took me in and I was grateful to see what a normal family looked like again. They spent time with me, talked to me, and gave me confidence in my athleticism. When I spent the night with them Mama Warrick would tuck me in and kiss my forehead. My gratitude towards them was and still is inexplicable. It sometimes took a village to raise my sister and me.

In the summer of 1980 our mobile home burned down and we couldn't salvage much. The firefighters said it took seven minutes to burn from end to end. I always thought it burned because we didn't keep it clean and therefore we were being punished by God for allowing it to be so despicable. I believed that so deeply that I couldn't put it out of my mind. We lost pictures, trophies, clothes, and just about everything we owned. It was yet another mortifying experience for our little family. I stayed with the Warrick's, Aunt Gail, and Mawmaw Bernice while Mama figured out where we were going to live. Mama and Joye stayed with Mama's friend Janice Emory. We were sometimes at the mercy of others. Thank God everyone that helped us were genuinely good people. We were so blessed.

Chapter 12- Free Lunch Kid

Mama used the insurance money from the fire to pay rent on another mobile home on busy Highway the busy highway to church or to our friend Kathryn Beam's house. 221. I never liked the new place. It wasn't on the hill and it wasn't home. Me and Joye used to walk up the road to our church friend Kathryn's house. She was around Mawmaw's age and her husband Charles went to school with Mawmaw. Joye had no fear and would walk on the road instead of beside it. She always worried me because she was so stubborn and just didn't seem to care about her own safety. Kathryn always welcomed us with open arms into her home and gladly fed us. That was a blessing for us two free lunch kids. She took us to church and was a magnificent influence on us. Her daughters Penny and Charleen became our friends too. We were blessed to have had great influences in our lives. God had a plan for us even in our darkness.

At the new place we didn't have a refrigerator. Years later Daddy told me that he felt bad because we didn't have a fridge and it worried him. We didn't have a phone either. I would go next door to the neighbors and use hers. That's where I called the police the first time in my life.

Mama's boyfriend was physically abusive to her. I would call the police and then I would hate to see them leave. Cops quickly became my heroes and I knew right away I wanted to be one when I grew up. He was a coward and ran off before the cops got there. It could have been that he was embarrassed to have gotten ran off by a 13 year old girl that was trying to protect her Mama. I had no problem trying to defend my Mama and sister. I didn't care about me. Once I came through the front door and Mama was on the floor behind the door. She still had on her blue green nightgown and she was bruised and hysterical. I confronted her boyfriend and he ran out the back door. It looked to me like he had tried to have sex with her.

Another time Joye was sitting in Mama's lap and Mama's boyfriend told her to get down. Mama told Joye not to get down and her boyfriend grabbed Mama's arm and started twisting it. I told him to stop because he was hurting her but he wouldn't. I intervened and blacked his eye and felt it squish. I remember him going to one of my high school basketball games with that black eye. I wasn't proud, I just felt weird about the whole incident.

Sometimes he would take Joye's things and hold them ransom until Mama paid him to give them back. Once he took Joye's beloved baseball glove and wouldn't give it back until somehow Mama got it back from him. Later on Joye and me were sitting in the car with a friend and she started talking about the baseball glove incident. I quickly hushed her to keep our darkness to ourselves.

Free Lunch Kid

I always prayed no one would see the "F" or "R" by my name.
But let me tell you I was always the first kid in line for school
breakfast and lunch.
It was hot and filling.
That was my normal.
At one point I walked home from school nightly about 3 miles.
I had to if I wanted to play basketball.
Because Mama didn't have the gas money to come and get me.
I never knew who was going to be there when I got home.
Always wondering if the electricity would be on.
Hoping Mama had not finally left for good like she regularly

threatened.
What would I do?
How would I take care of my sister?
She didn't deserve this.
Where would we go?
That was my normal.
Our first step daddy drank a lot but he wasn't mean.
They argued a lot but never violently.
They divorced.
Then there was the crazy maker.
I was 13.
Mama was 29.
I think he was 19.
Don't know.
Don't care.
We lived in a small run down trailer.
I came home from school one day to find that
mama had tried to kill herself for the first time.
The first of many attempts- too many to count.
She was sick of him and I was convinced that she hated us.
She hated herself.
There was violence in our home.
I came home from school one day and she was lying on the
floor.
Screaming to the top of her lungs.

It looked to me like she had been beat up.
She was bruised and battered.
I remember she still had her nightgown on.
It was blue green.
When he heard me come in he ran out the back door and into the
woods.
I chased him impulsively.
I don't know why he ran so hard from a 13 year old free lunch
kid.

Chapter 13- GED

In 1981, Mama applied and was accepted to a program at Isothermal Community College in our hometown. It was called the Human Resources Development Program (HRDP) and it was Monday through Friday, eight hours a day. She got paid $80.00 a week. It was like a regular job except they taught job skills and helped her get her GED! She finished high school. We were proud of her and she was proud of herself. She was working towards becoming a teacher assistant at Harris Elementary School where I went and Joye was still attending. Her studies were in Early Childhood Education. Mama was highly intelligent and could have excelled at anything she wanted to when her not yet diagnosed mental illness would let her. She wanted to do more and be more. She wanted to give us a good life and really help others. She often tried very hard but there was a cloud of doom that would rear its horrid head and it was relentless.

Chapter 14- The First of Many & H707119 Appears

The new place never felt like home. I longed for my country place on the hill. There I could see the Smokey Mountains in the distance and the rolling hills behind our 1.7 acre property would greet me like an old familiar friend. The new place was on a highway that was full of trucks and speeding cars. The noise of the traffic was unsettling and made an already anxious me secretly more nervous in general. There was a diner down the road and a phone booth in its parking lot. From time to time if I could scrape up some change, I would walk down there and use the phone. Usually I would call Daddy or my school friend, teammate, and role model Lori Toney. I looked up to Lori and she was a positive force in my life. I was fortunate to have influences outside our home that believed in me even though I loathed myself.

Mama made me take the tiny bedroom and gave Joye the bigger bedroom. She said I didn't keep my room clean so I had to take the little room. That was true. I didn't keep my room clean. I didn't know how. That doesn't make sense but it was true. My undiagnosed anxiety grew. Our home life was jacked up, out of control, and nose diving.

I began to write poetry. Most of my writing was awfully dark. At times I felt like my own suicide was the only way I would get any relief. I believed that if I was gone then Mama would be happier too. Maybe her life would be easier if I hadn't come along and messed it up. I felt I was responsible for her misery by being born. She continued to tell me she hated me and to go to hell. She told me I was the reason her life was so bad. Writing and excelling in sports kept me alive and kept me in school. Sometimes I would daydream about how I could disappear. I thought that was what Mama wanted. I know now that she wasn't in her right mind and couldn't be rational. Mama's love for me and my sister was hiding behind the mask of an undiagnosed mental illness. She adored us but her adoration was being trumped by demons she could not shake. A dark passenger was now riding shotgun with her everywhere she went. Her decision making went from awful to mortifying. Life was hell on earth for those of us in her household. Food was scarce and Joye and I never knew when the electricity would be cut off.

She loved us unconditionally but the mental illness stalker was in charge most of the time. In the midst of chaos, drama, and trauma there were glimpses of kindness and tenderness. In 1981, Christmas came and Mama had just started a new job. Money was always scarce and the stress it caused on Mama was pitiful at times. Every Christmas of our lives she always had us a stocking a piece. They were filled with our favorite candy, gum, tiny toys, and whatever else she could afford to buy. In fact she gave us both a Christmas stocking every year and many years after we became adults.

She knew I had an affinity for photographs and that I had always wanted a camera. When we unwrapped our gifts that year Mama gave me a camera. I loved it and she was thrilled to be able to give it to me. At her new job she was able to pick out a small gift from their catalog and as the higher power would have it a camera was in that catalog. She chose it and wrapped it just for me. She also knew Joye loved to cook. Mama bought and individually wrapped up cake mixes for Joye to open. She also wrote us an IOU letter that Christmas. She promised to make it up to us and have a better Christmas even if it was in July. July came and went but Mama meant well.

Then the bottom fell completely out of our lives as if we were tethered together and thrown off the top of Chimney Rock. Not too long after we moved to the new place in 1981, Mama attempted suicide for the first time. She took a bunch of pills. It was hell. Oh my God. What do we do now? Joye and me were beside ourselves. What were we going to do? Mama became known as H707119. That was her Rutherford County Hospital ID number that she would use many, many times from that moment on and over the span of her life.

I accept now as an adult the emotional battle between mothers and teenage daughters, but it was more than that. It was verbal abuse almost daily. The neglect and fears of abandonment were a nonstop and constant struggle. Mama used to tell me that if I was not happy at her house then I should call my Daddy to come and get me and go live with him. She would say "go pack your shit up and go live with your Daddy if you don't like it here." She used that as leverage when things would go wrong. Her consistent threats were like bullets aimed directly at me and impossible to avoid or deflect. I had no armor. I was a child. We had very little structure or regular discipline. When she did try to correct us or discipline us it was a challenge for all parties involved. She would scream and yell thinking that would get her the results she wanted. She would swing whatever was near her, belt, flip flop, coat hanger or her dreaded left hand. Joye and I were acutely aware of the fact that she was a lefty and we would sometimes get slapped on the right side of the head or face. Bobbing and weaving was a learned defense mechanism. Her irrational onslaught of threats became too much for me to take. She told me to leave one time too many. One day I took her up on that and I packed my shit up and moved in with my Daddy. I was 14. I don't recall her ever asking me to come home. That was a decision that may have saved my life but I live with regret for leaving Joye to this day.

After I left Mama's house for good, and on two different occasions, Mama and Joye fled the house and went over to a neighbors. On one of those nights Mama went to the ER due to chest and nose injuries. I didn't get it back then, but I had left my little sister in hell and I couldn't forgive myself. Still haven't and doubt I will.

No Man No Money

She sits alone trying
to read the big print.
Her phone don't ring and the
kids don't show.
It's the middle of the month
and her money is low.
Her friends are losers
but her pills are winners.
She wonders why
she's still a sinner.
She blinks her eyes
And now she is old.
For the love of a man
She sold her soul.
She ran her kids out
And chose him first.
A woman like her
is really the worst.
She'll be sitting alone
and lonely as hell.
She looks in the mirror
and she starts to yell.
She knows the reasons why
but she just can't cope.
The end of the line
There is no hope.
Her days are all dark.
It'll never be sunny.
Cause she's got no man and
She's got no money.

Chapter 15- Gastric Bypass

Mama was overweight and needed help losing it. In 1981 she weighed 254 lbs. and was 5'9" tall. She was desperate to shed some pounds. Her self-esteem was directly tied to her weight and having an undiagnosed mental illness didn't help. She decided to have gastric bypass surgery. It was a new procedure that worked. Mama was finally able to know what it felt like to be slim. She looked amazing. It was obvious that she felt better about herself. Her self-esteem was at an all-time high.

Unfortunately the surgery caused her to become bulimic. That became a long term problem for her. She still over ate which caused her stomach to stretch more than it was supposed to. She gradually gained some of her weight back but the bulimia stayed with her for many years following that surgery. She eventually stopped throwing up and was able to put that behind her. It took about 30 years to go away but the damage it caused didn't. The bypass surgery would come into play again and cause her some health issues more than once. The vomiting aided in eroding her teeth prematurely. She also battled Irritable Bowel Syndrome daily partially due to the gastric bypass. It would also cause future gastrointestinal tests to be impossible to do.

Mawmaw came up from Rock Hill to help take care of Mama while she recuperated from surgery. But Mama had other plans. She and her boyfriend decided to go to the beach. While there they decided to stay. Just like that. Mawmaw, her sister in-law, and me ended up moving Mama and Joye's belongings out of their apartment back home. Mama wasn't too concerned about their belongings because she knew at the end of the day Mawmaw and me would save her. She was living in the moment and leaving her responsibilities for Mawmaw to clean up again.

Joye went to the beach to be with Mama. She was on her own too much because Mama wasn't around. Joye ran that beach from Springmaid Beach to the end of Ocean Boulevard. She was 11 years old and should have never been left alone to roam whenever and whenever she wanted to. Once that summer I grabbed a ride to the beach with a church member to visit Mama and Joye. When I got there I started walking Ocean Boulevard looking for Joye. Through the enormous body to body summer crowd I saw her in the distance. She was making her some money by handing out flyers for an arcade. She was way too young to be talking to hundreds of strangers. She had no fear factor and was still stubborn as an old mule.

She was by herself often and stayed with neighbors they had just met. She wanted to continue going to Harris Elementary School back home. So at the end of that summer she left Mama and her beloved Myrtle Beach behind and came to live with me and Daddy.

That was a tough time for Joye. She was Mama's baby girl and being rejected and not taken care of by Mama was just awful for her. She was angry and in pain. Daddy and I loved her but we were not Mama. When I turned 16 and got my license I took her to school daily. In the afternoon she rode the bus from Harris Elementary School to Chase High School where I was in the 11th grade. She would hang out while I practiced softball. When practice was over me and her would drive back to Daddy's in his raggedy ole orange Plymouth Duster (AKA punkin') together. We tried to move on but truthfully we were pitiful.

Eventually Mama moved back to Forest City, NC, and Joye moved back in with her. Mama started seeing a new guy and he was super nice. He was a good person and adored her. For whatever reason she pushed "the good" away. She eventually started staying away from home and left Joye with the new guy. When she was home she and Joye didn't get along anymore. Joye was growing up and she needed her Mama but Mama was just not there physically or emotionally. She was taking her anger out on Joye. She would try to discipline her by swinging a belt at her including the buckle. Joye hit back at Mama a few times because she couldn't take it anymore. Mama was home less and less. One time Joye got scared and tried to get Mama to come home but she wouldn't. The next day Joye called me and my friend Missy to come and get her and we took her to Daddy's. Mama ran off to the beach again and Missy and me stayed with Joye. She never lived with Mama again after that and their relationship would never be the same.

Joye had to sleep on the couch because I was a selfish ass. That meant she couldn't go to bed until everyone else did. We had a roof over our heads though and we knew Daddy loved us. He was brand new at the full time dad gig but he gave it his best. Joye only stayed with us a few months. Mama moved back from the beach and Joye lived with her 3 more years. Joye moved back in with Daddy when she was 15.

I had started staying away from Daddy's pretty often. I stayed with school friends, teammates, church friends, and finally the Limerick's. I met Missy Limerick at my first real job waiting tables at the local Shoney's Restaurant in the fall of 1983. Missy and I hit it off right away. She helped train me and get me ready to serve customers. I still played sports all the time but I needed to make some money to better care for myself. I also needed my own transportation to get myself from school and back since I lived out of district. I had my eye on a pearl blue Honda TwinStar 200 motorcycle. I eventually got that bike and I loved it. Working at Shoney's provided me the opportunity to get the bike, meet new friends, and learn a life lesson about how hard waiting tables can be. I had to wear a brown polyester dress and I only got one. We didn't have a dryer at Daddy's so I would wash it and wear it to work wet. No one could tell because it was dark and the material was thick.

I eventually moved in with the Limerick's in late winter of 1984. I stayed with them off and on for the next several years. They welcomed me and I got close to Missy's mama, Liz, very quickly. I finally had a sense of a little stability again and I knew for sure I was loved. I was very much loved! I was finally as happy as a very emotionally immature, anxiety ridden, barely seventeen year old emotionally abused girl could be. I was successful in sports and was preparing to play ball in college and I was finally loved again. Between Missy, her Mama Liz, and their crazy large family, I figured out I maybe wanted to live and that maybe I deserved love. I was not unworthy!

In 1985, Joye moved in with a friend of Mama's. She stayed there about two years. While there she had a minor motorcycle accident and banged her knee up pretty good. She had to have an outpatient scar tissue removal surgery. The surgery was successful however she developed a life threatening staph infection. She was in the hospital a total of 6 weeks. At one point we had to put on sterile clothes to visit her. Her temperature spiked to 106 and her weight got down to 95 pounds. It was scary to say the least. She would eventually have 13 surgeries on that same knee including 5 knee replacements. The first one would be at the very young age of 30.

Joye was originally in Rutherford Hospital but after a couple of weeks they released her even though she had a high temperature. That same day Mama took her to Spartanburg Hospital where she was admitted and remained for 4 more weeks. Mama had a psychiatrist visit Joye because she seemed depressed. That was because she was! She was 16, couldn't walk, and her Mama was a flake. The psychiatrist gave Joye some medicine for depression. Joye spit it out and Mama grabbed the pills and kept them for herself.

During the course of Joye's stay in the hospital Mama visited a young patient she had met in the Psychiatric Unit during her own previous stay at Spartanburg Hospital. She had had a relationship with him. She met him in the psychiatric unit while they were both patients and she hooked up with him. He was 21 and Mama was 36.

Sister pain deep as mine
Fading back in the hands of time
Stomachs growl but hearts growl louder
Outstretched arms-no hug no power
Heads stayed dropped-the walk is slow
Shake my head because I know
The little girls that lived through hell
Watch out now we have a story to tell

Chapter 16- Bull Street Via Spartanburg

From 1981-1986 Mama attempted suicide 7 times and had her stomach pumped and or Ipecac (vomit inducing liquid) was administered each time. On October 11, 1986 when Mama was 37 years old she tried to commit suicide again. Her medical records show the county police was contacted about a possible overdose. That time she had taken an overdose of a high blood pressure medication called Inderal. She was 5'9" tall and weighed 167 pounds. She had been living with a different new boyfriend for about a year and a half in Inman, SC. He was a decent guy but Mama usually ran the "decent" away. In her words she attempted suicide to "get away from everything."

Her Medical Records state that her mental status on admit was:

Her affect is mildly constricted and towards the depressed side of the scale (affect is a psychological term for observable expression of emotion). She is not psychotic, delusional, and no hallucinations. She is reacting to psychosocial stress factors and appears to have problems with pathological dependency needs.

Past history: 7 suicide attempts in the last 7 years.

She was placed on the closed end of the Psychiatric Unit and given Xanax (anti-anxiety). 5mg., Motrin, Parafin orte (muscle relaxer), Tryptophan (mood swings), Doxepin (sleep aid), and Sinequan (anti-depressant). Due to cooperation and rapid improvement, the patient was transferred to the open unit on 10/13/86. Her symptoms worsened when Doxepin was increased. She was able to go on a successful day trip with her current boyfriend.

The patient is somewhat overly flirtatious and dependent on this admission and appeared to latch onto a 21 year old personality disorder patient. (That is the guy she fooled around with when Joye was a patient). She seemed to be playing him against her current boyfriend. Patient was highly manipulative during this admission and appeared to be setting her boyfriend up for a rescue situation. He apparently has no insight on her personality disorder. By 10/28/86 she appeared to be ready for discharge into an outpatient setting.

ADMITTING   DIAGNOSIS:

AXIS   I: Adjustment disorder (difficulty adjusting to change or stress) with depressed mood. Rule out affective disorder (depression, bipolar, and anxiety).

AXIS   II: Rule out personality disorder (a deeply ingrained and manipulative pattern of behavior).

AXIS III: Past history of 4 suicide attempts. Status posts multiple surgeries with tonsillectomy and adenoidectomy at 21 years of age. Status post hysterectomy at 22 years of age. Status post abdominal bypass surgery 4 years ago. Mild obesity. Mild right lower quadrant abdominal pain on exam.

DISCHARGE DIAGNOSIS:

AXIS I: Overdose of inderal (blood pressure medicine). Rule out dysthymic affective disorder (experience little or no joy), blunted TRH (thyroid) test on this admission.

AXIS II: Personality disorder, mixed type with borderline personality being the most prominent. The patient does have prominent and dependent (depends on others to meet emotional needs) passive-aggressive traits. Somatization disorder (experiencing physical symptoms that cannot be explained by an identifiable medical condition) with prominent hypochondrial features along with generalized anxiety disorder.

AXIS III: See AXIS II list above.

AXIS IV: Psychosocial stress factors, level 4, moderate.

AXIS V: Highest level of adaptive functioning past year, level 4, fair.

10/12/86 (day after admitted)

PATIENT NUMBER 826522

AGE 37

Admission Notes and Psychological/Social Report

PRESENTING PROBLEM: The primary problem is related to depression. The onset

of this difficulty was between two and five years ago. This problem occurs several times a day and has had a significant effect on her everyday life. In addition to the primary problem, Ms. Robbins is also plagued by difficulties associated with family, loneliness, moodiness, self-confidence, physical state, and sex life.

FAMILY AND DEVELOPMENT HISTORY: Ms. Robbins was raised primarily by her natural parents. In retrospect she describes her childhood as being hard to remember. Mother was characterized as warm, strict, fault finding, and affectionate. She describes her father as strict, domineering, faultfinding, and affectionate. Characteristics of her parents' relationship were given as follows: ambivalent and loving. There were no other children in the family. She was an only child. As a child, Ms. Robbins was characteristically friendly, emotional, nervous, and stubborn. The following problems occurred in childhood: excessive fears or worries, academic, feeling a burden to parents, overweight, hurt feelings, and fear of failure. Parents argued about money, relatives, and jealousy. As a child Ms. Robbins father and mother worked primarily as unskilled laborers. Mother's method of discipline is described as fairly strict and fathers as strict. Childhood fears included: failing and being laughed at. Sexual experiences have been reported to have been mutual.

EDUCATION: Ms. Robbins reports that she received a GED. The self-rating of intellectual ability is average. She has never repeated a grade. Grades were usually C's. She does not recall ever getting into trouble at school. Learning to read was not a problem. In learning math she encountered problems. Compared to other children, Ms. Robbins feels that she was more often the brunt of teasing and ridicule than were other children.

FINANCIAL HISTORY AND STATUS: Economic status during childhood and adolescence is rated within the working class. The major source of family income came from the father. In deciding on how the family's money was to be spent, there were disagreements at times between parents. Finances were occasionally a source of family problems. Currently Ms. Robbins's household is supported by an income of $8,000-$12,000. She reports a significant reduction in income during the last two years. Family income is derived primarily from her partner's income. Providing enough income is an important stressor.

EMPLOYMENT HISTORY: She is currently unemployed. She has been dismissed by an employer on at least one occasion. Ms. Robbins did lose work when laid off by an employer. The greatest length of employment in one position was for a period of three to five years. Since beginning work on a full time basis she has gone unemployed for a period of six months to a year. The following vocations have been pursued in the past: homemaker, salesperson, and an unskilled worker.

ALCOHOL AND DRUG HISTORY: Regarding past drug use the following was reported: amphetamines and marijuana. A report of using alcohol to excess on several occasions was acquired. Ms. Robbins says that she uses alcohol once a month, and uses illegal drugs once or twice a year. Past involvement for drug abuse or alcohol abuse was denied. While growing up her caretakers did not have a drinking problem. Regarding the use of tobacco, she reports that she has never used cigarettes.

MEDICAL HISTORY: No close relatives are reported to have disturbing mental illness. She did remember that she did have a serious illness as a child but she did not elaborate. In the past three years Ms. Robbins has been involved in at least one accident and has not had any major illness. General level of health is rated as fair. Currently she is not under the care of a doctor.

MARITAL AND FAMILY LIFE: In regards to marital status, she is separated. She has been involved in her current relationship for two years. Ms. Robbins is the parent of two children. Behavioral problems are reported to be an issue in child rearing. She describes her partner as warm, unhappy, boring, tense, and affectionate. At present she does not live with relatives, friends, nor live in own home, dorm, or boarding house. Arguments with her partner are alleged to occur several times a week. The current relationship has never been threatened by an affair. Shared interests in his relationship include sports, movies, socializing with friends, television, and talking. The partner is evaluated as fulfilling his role fairly well.

DIET AND EXERCISE: In regards to eating habits Ms. Robbins does not eat a balanced diet nor does she exercise. She is currently a little overweight.

PSYCHOLOGICAL AND SOCIAL STRESSORS: In the past two years Ms. Robbins has experienced the following stressful events and circumstances: fired at work and change in number of arguments with partner. The following stressful events and circumstances also occurred during this same period: death of a close friend (Gail Sisk Powell Reid), change in financial state, and personal injury or illness.

Regarding legal involvement, she has been implicated in civil matters. Current ability to cope with existing stressors is rated as poor. The following characteristics were chosen as being self-descriptive: outgoing, talkative, aggressive, temperamental, friendly, smart, impatient. The descriptors selected to portray her current mental state are as follows: tense, depressed, sad, worried, fearful, angry, irritable, and distrustful.

HISTORY AND PHYSICAL CHIEF COMPLAINT:"I have been feeling depressed lately and wanted to take my life".

HISTORY OF PRESENT ILLNESS: Patient is a 37 year old white female who has been admitted for an overdose of Inderal. She was seen in the emergency room as an attempted suicide. She has multiple suicide attempts in the past five years. All attempts have been p.o. (oral) overdoses, at this present time being Inderal and one of the previous attempts being Fiorinal (muscle relaxer). She was divorced in 1975 and remarried in 1977. She separated from her second husband in 1979. That divorce is not yet final. She has been living with a boyfriend here in Spartanburg County after moving from a friend's apartment where she helped care for a who child who had an illness. They eventually had problems and an argument ensued. She left and the friend would not let her get inside to get any of her belongings.

She does report conflicts with her current boyfriend. He is in love with her but she is not with him. She also has impaired relationships with her daughters. One is twenty and lives in Asheville. The other daughter is sixteen and lives with somebody she thought was her best friend. She is separated from and has little interactions with her family. She is an only child and her father is deceased from a heart attack. Her mother is living and has hypertension and arthritis.

The exam included a complete physical and checked skin, eyes, neck, lungs, heart, abdomen, extremities, and genitals, pelvic, skeletal, and neurological.

Chapter 17- Bull Street Incident

On January 6, 1987 Mama was shipped to the infamous South Carolina State Mental Hospital on Bull Street in Columbia, SC. Her doctor at Spartanburg Hospital referred her there. Attempting suicide in South Carolina wasn't a crime. However it seemed as though it was treated like one. It wasn't an arrest but she was taken into protective custody for her own safety. Even though she was referred and it was a voluntary admit, Mama was taken to Bull Street via police car. Joye had a heated discussion with the   police officer. She told him she didn't want Mama sent there in a police car. She also proceeded to tell the officer that if he took Mama via police car he would have to take her too. He said ok then! Joye quickly decided to let him take Mama in the police car. She followed them. So there it was. Mama was headed to the state hospital and 16 year old Joye drove behind the cop car for that long hour drive to Bull St. Dammit! That was something Joye should NEVER have had to do! Mama's doctor told me I should be glad Joye didn't get locked up for pitching such a fit with the police officer. My response was yall shouldn't have taken Mama via police car then.

When the South Carolina State Hospital opened in 1828, its name was the South Carolina Lunatic Asylum. It had a reputation for housing some of the most violent and criminally insane patients in existence. It was enormous yet often over- crowded and patients sometimes slept in hallways. The campus was diverse and a mini-city in of itself. It had everything from a movie theatre to a full lockdown ward. There was a mattress factory, churches, and at one point they even made their own electricity. During the Civil War it was used as a prisoner of war camp. That place was bigger than life and quite intimidating.

Upon admission her evaluation was as follows:

AXIS 1:Major depression, recurrent bulimia

AXIS II: Rule out borderline personality (reckless and impulsive behavior) disorder.

AXIS III: Migraine headaches, low back pain, hypotension   by   history. Medications: Sinequan fordepression, Parafon forte for muscle tension   headache Midrin
and *Maxside for migraines.*

Psychological consult was obtained andt showed features ofdepressive disorder prominent dependent and passive-aggressive personality features operating at a rathe r borderline level of organization.

PSYCHOLOGICAL EVALUATION 1/26/87

Barbara Robbins is referred for evaluation by Dr. Elkashef for assistance in determining the extent of depressive traits and the likelihood of a borderline personality disorder. Mrs. Robbins is a 37 year old separated white female referred from Spartanburg Mental Health Center with recurrent episodes of depression and two suicide attempts since October, 1986.

Mrs. Robbins is a neatly and cleanly dressed woman who appeared to be her stated age. She related in a very subdued manner throughout, reflecting low energy, almost to the point of inertia (sluggish, inactivity, tendency to do nothing, remain unchanged). Her voice became progressively lower and her facial expression progressively downtrodden. Though the rate and flow of her speech was adequate, the mood reflected in other ways gave her a very depressed, lethargic look. She was well oriented in all spheres, and gave no overt indication of looseness that would be associated with thought disorder. She related that she had been depressed for many years. She described that she was an only child and very lonely in her formative years because her family "lived out in the sticks". She was married at the age of sixteen, had her first child at seventeen, miscarried at nineteen, had her second daughter at twenty one, and divorced at twenty four. Her father also died when she was twenty four. She remarried at twenty seven and separated two years later. She is still in that separation as she and her second husband have not yet divorced. In July of this year she lost her job and her apartment.

Mrs. Robbins related that she was first suicidal in 1981 at which time she took a Tylenol overdose. She related that her stomach was pumped and or she has taken Ipecac about six times in the last six years. Her children, ages twenty and seventeen have each lived with their father since they were fifteen. She related in a very downtrodden manner that, "I've not been the greatest parent." She also related with a very helpless air that "I don't know where I belong." She now feels herself to be under pressure from two men. One with whom she has lived with for some time and one with whom she has had an affair since October when she met him as a former patient in her previous psychiatric hospitalization in Spartanburg. (He was the twenty year old patient she started seeing when Joye was hospitalized with her knee injury).

45

She was administered the Millon Clinical Multiaxial Inventory (MCMI) (psychological assessment tool to help provide information on psychiatric disorders) and the Rorschach (psychological inkblot test where subject is asked to describe). These test data revealed a person who is extensively both dependent and passive-aggressive in basic character makeup who is so poorly functional that she is exhibiting some secondary borderline features. The dependent aspects of her borderline adaptation are consistent with what she describes as a long history of parental overprotection and isolation in childhood, leading to an unusual attachment to, and dependency on some caretaking figure. She has an extensive sense of inadequacy and incompetence which pervades her every remark and look. She has accentuated these weaknesses by avoiding responsibility and clinging to others. This has restricted her opportunity to learn skills for taking care of herself. She really has not done very well in terms of handling the separation required of growing up. She has apparently gone from one intense attachment to another. The earlier separations created tense anxiety and have been instrumental in bringing about mood fluctuations, self-condemnation, and guilt. She seems to consistently place herself in very vulnerable positions in her relationships with others. As she clings to others and avoids autonomy, she eventually exasperates those on whom she depends and ends up losing their support. Her moods are largely based upon either marked self-reproach or rather frantic efforts to gain attention from others. This will mark her wide and intense mood swings.

She also shows a number of passive-aggressive personality features at a borderline level of adaptation. This will lead her to be rather negativistic, discontented, and erratic in a way that she deals with others. She has learned to anticipate a great deal of disappointment and at times will alienate others before they reject her. She remarked that her mother has told her that she has never stayed with any of the people who have treated her best. Mrs. Robbins remarked, "I guess I just try to hurt others before they can hurt me." There is a great deal of inner tension and difficulty regulating her emotions which keeps her churning very close to the surface and leads her to act impulsively and with little deliberation. This will result in conflict with other people and make it hard to develop affectionate and intimate relationships. She seems to be a very grim, angry, and rather pessimistic person and at times is likely to be rather explosive in a bitter kind of way as she sees the world having delivered very little for her. At other times she may turn against herself, at which time she is likely to be just as impulsively self-damaging.

Overall, she shows many of the features of a depressive disorder with prominent dependent and passive-aggressive personality features operating at a rather borderline level of organization.

HOSPITAL COURSE:

Mrs. Robbins was started on Sinequan 75 mgs. and gradually increased to 150 mgs. at h.s. (hour of sleep or bedtime) with gradual improvement of her depressive symptomatology. It was then increased to 200 mg. Clinically she continued to show improvement in mood, sleep pattern, and involvement in activities and better self-esteem. It was decided not to increase the dose of the antidepressant. Regarding the diagnosis of bulimia the patient had gained weight on admission. Her weight was 159 on admission and she went up to 178 lbs. Her weight then fluctuated 5 pounds. She reported two to three episodes of bingeing and purging per week with no medical complication.

The patient has been tried on multiple weekend passes with variable results. She had terminated the relationship with her boyfriend during this admission without regression. She was observed during the admission to test limits frequently and engaging in inappropriate displays of affection with male patients. She was also found to require much limit setting and lost privileges often due to noncompliance with the rules and poor attendance to activity groups. She participated in individual supportive therapy. In the last few weeks of admission, she was placed on boarding status. Complete resolution of depressive symptoms was observed. We dealt mainly with her placement problems. She was referred to Killingsworth and was interviewed and accepted. She was also working with vocational rehabilitation and went on some job interviews.

CONDITION ON DISCHARGE:

The patient was discharged in an improved condition with resolution of depressive symptomatology; no suicidal or homicidal ideation. Her bingeing and purging behavior had somewhat persisted and correlated with her emotional state and body weight. She is medically stable.

DISCHARGE MEDICATIONS:

The patient is discharged on Sinequan (nerve pain and antidepressant), Midrin (migraines), Maxzide (diuretic). Two weeks supply of medications was given. Patient is aware of possible side effects of medications and potential complications of her eating disorder.

DISCHARGE AND FOLLOW UP ARRANGEMENTS:

The patient was discharged to Killingsworth Halfway House on March 18, 1987. She has a follow up appointment at the Columbia Area Mental Health Clinic on March 27, 1987 at 10:30. She is also to schedule an appointment with her family physician on her own for follow up of the associated medical problems. PROCEDURES: None.

FINAL DIAGNOSIS:

AXIS I: Major depression, recurrent bulimia

AXIS II: Mixed personality disorder with dependent and passive-aggressive trait

AXIS III: Migraine headaches, hypotension

Psychological consult was obtained and it showed features of depressive disorder with prominent dependent and passive-aggressive personality features operating at a rather borderline level of organization.

Chapter 18-The Halfway House

On March 18, 1987 Mama was discharged from William S. Hall Institute (Hall) to go to Killingsworth Halfway House for women. The plan was arranged and paid for by Vocational Rehabilitation. She was there for three weeks. While there she had little motivation to look for a job, voiced multiple somatic complaints (imagined pain but feels real), and spent most of the day "socializing" at Hall institute where several friends remained hospitalized.

On Saturday April 4, 1987 she signed out of Killingsworth for an overnight trip and was scheduled to return the next evening. It was learned that she went to the beach with some friends, all of whom were former Hall Institute patients. One was said to be her current boyfriend she had met at Hall Institute. From the beach they proceeded to Rockingham, NC, where one of the men had family residing. The man allegedly broke into one of his sister's homes and stole some jewelry. He proceeded to leave his traveling companions stranded.

On Monday night April 6, 1987 Mama called Mawmaw and explained her situation. Mawmaw reported that Mama spoke of being depressed and of taking too much medication. That was later confirmed by a friend in NC with whom she had spoken with. Mama had actually taken twenty Sinequan (antidepressant) and somehow got to Mawmaw's in Rock Hill, SC. Joye drove the hour and 45 minute drive to Mawmaw's and picked Mama up and took her back to Columbia. Mama had missed her doctor's appointment and tried to get herself admitted back at Hall Institute via the Columbia Area Mental Health Center Emergency Room. According to the mental health center consultant's write up, the doctor on call at William S. Hall Psychiatric Institute had her sent directly to the state hospital instead. It was determined the admission at the State Hospital would be more appropriate considering the circumstance.

Tentative discharge plans:
According to Killingsworth, she cannot return there. The staff there learned that Mama had spoken of killing herself. Vocational Rehabilitation views the patient's efforts to find employment and a regular income as superficial. Vocational Rehabilitation will likely re-evaluate the feasibility of financing another such venture. Mrs. Robbins has no source of income and has not determined to be eligible for disability benefits. She does not have any confirmed living arrangement. Alternate placement is indicated but there is no plan in place at present.

PSYCOSOCIAL ASSESSMENT

TREATMENT/RECOMMENDATIONS: Mrs. Robbins appears to manage her life in a very irresponsible and superficial manner. This attitude encompasses personal relationships, employment opportunities, and prescribed treatment for her mental and emotional disorders. Impulse control, judgment, and insight are seen as poor. Recommend stabilization on medication, patient education, and a living skills group program. The patient might also benefit from groups that focus on problem solving and stress management.

Chapter 19- One Flew Over Bull Street

Killingsworth was done with her. It was official. Mama was involuntarily committed to the South Carolina State Mental Hospital on April 8, 1987.

She called me hysterically crying, pleading, and begging me to get her out of there. I had heard that cry for help before. "Help me Rob. Get me out of here. Please help me." I was 21 years old. Those words were spoken to me quite a few times throughout our lives. Most of the time I could help her, but that time she was locked up and there was literally nothing I could do. We had to wait for her hearing. I remember Mawmaw being worried, hurt, and confused for Mama. That was new territory for our family and we were devastated yet again.

My friend Missy and me headed down to Columbia. That day would forever be etched into our brains. The word "Columbia" would eternally be synonymous with the Bull Street incident. Upon arrival to that larger than life mental institute, we stepped out of the car and it was the kind of thick hot heat that felt like stepping into hell. Maybe we were. Missy later told me that moment broke her heart and caused her to look at me and wonder what I must be feeling. She said I seemed as if I was going to visit a friend in the hospital not my Mama in a locked down involuntary admit to a mental institute. She told me I always seemed normal to her. I didn't cry or feel sorry for myself. She said I didn't seem afraid. She had no idea back then what mental illness was like but she did understand that my lack of emotion was a considerable oddity to her. Little did she know my lifelong gift of compartmentalizing was showing off that day!

We went up and visited Mama and I immediately knew she didn't belong there or at least on that floor. It was like a television movie. We were patted down to ensure we didn't have any contraband on us. The wing she was on was secured by a heavy steel door and we had to be escorted and buzzed into Ward 118 on floor 120. The patients on her floor were very obviously mentally ill. It was like a scene from One Flew Over The Coo Coo's Nest. Mama had an odd obsessive compulsive action. She consistently pinched and rubbed in the bend of her arms until they bruised. She did that when she was anxious or stressed. Her arms looked so bad and she was so very ashamed and demeaned. There were two people to a room. Mama's roommate was pitiful but Mama was sweet and comforting to her. That didn't surprise us though because no matter what Mama was going through she was compassionate towards others. Like so many times before, when we left I honestly didn't know if that was the last time I would see my Mama alive. Hope was a fleeting word that was challenging to believe in or hold on to.

Since Mama was committed she had to stay thirty days and then appear before a judge. The judge would then determine her release or further involuntary stay. Since she had nowhere to go, was indigent, and basically homeless, and as a result of her actions on April 21, 1987 she was judicially committed. Mawmaw couldn't let Mama move in with her. It was just too much. Mama literally had nowhere to go. Joye said the look on Mama's face was unforgettable when the judge committed her. Mama had never been arrested but that sort of felt like an arrest. She had done a lot of things but stealing, lying, drinking, drugs, or anything else that might get her arrested was not one of them. But there she was, locked up as if she was being incarcerated for being sick!

DATES OF HOSPITALIZATION

Admitted Ward 120 4/8/87.

Discharged 6/18/87

CIRCUMSTANCES SURROUNDING ADMISSION: This is the second admission for this thirty seven year old white female admitted as an emergency from Richland County April 8, 1987. She was judicially committed by the probate court on April 21, 1987.

HISTORY AND PHYSICAL EXAMINATION: Patient has a history of a major depressive disorder and has had one previous admission to William S. Hall Psychiatric Institute in January of 1987. She was discharged in March, 1987. On her present admission patient showed impaired reasoning and judgment. She was cooperative and neat in appearance and stated that she felt that she was under a lot of stress with her old boyfriend harassing her. Her memory was intact and she was oriented to all three spheres (person, place, date/time). Her physical condition was essentially within normal limits.

PROVISIONAL DIAGNOSIS: Rule out borderline personality disorder. Rule out bulimia. Rule out major depression, recurrent.

COURSE OF HOSPITALIZATION AND TREATMENT: The patient is placed on antidepressant medication and slowly began to show improvement in her medical condition. She also has a history of bulimia and anorexia nervosa. She had a previous gastric stapling due to obesity and was found to have a Vitamin B12 deficiency for which we treated. The patient responded well to therapy and after two and a half months of treatment the patient had reached maximum hospital benefits and further hospitalization was not indicated.

FINAL DIAGNOSIS: AXIS I: Major depression, recurrent, anorexia nervosa, bulimia

AXIS II: Mixed personality disorder with passive aggressive and dependent features

AXIS III: Vitamin B12 deficiency Status post gastrostomy

RECOMMENDATIONS: The patient was granted a discharge on June 18, 1987 and will reside in West Columbia, SC. She will receive follow up care at the Lexington Mental Health Center. She left the hospital on Norpramin 100 mgs. at bedtime, Vistaril 50 mgs. Every morning and 100 mgs. at bedtime and Vitamin B12, 1000 micrograms I.M. every two weeks.

Out of the blue Mama's childhood best friend AKA Aunt Patsy called Mawmaw Betty to check on Mama. Aunt Patsy had dreamed that Mama died. It seemed so real and she couldn't get Mama off of her mind. Mawmaw reassured Patsy that Mama was alive but just barely. Somehow Aunt Patsy knew Mama was in trouble. Their connection was unbreakable. Neither miles nor years ever changed their unconditional love for each other.

It is my eyes looking back at me
But it is her that I always see
She is heavy and so is her heart
Her children and her are far apart
Away in miles as far as the sun
Running a race that can never be won
So she lays at home and lies on her tongue
Wishing she could go back to where it begun.

Chapter 20- Sin Coat

Mama was discharged from Bull Street on June 18, 1987. She stayed in Columbia and moved in with her second abuser. She met him at William S. Hall Psychiatric Institute while they were both patients. On holidays I would drive to Columbia to pick her up and take her to Mawmaw's in Forest City, NC. Mawmaw had moved from Rock Hill, SC back to our Home place in 1988. After a brief visit I would take her back to Columbia, SC. Mama liked it there and worked as a van driver for a medical transport company. She would take people to their doctor appointments. She loved helping others.

They didn't have a car and she would sometimes take the bus. I never looked at women at bus stops the same way after that. I noticed them more often and I would stare at the women waiting for the bus regardless of where I was. I was curious about where they were going and why they didn't have a car. Were they poor and hopeless or doing fine but liked taking the bus?

She wanted to make her life there but unfortunately her new boyfriend was an old gangster dude with a rap sheet. He had a violent temper and he ensured he ruled Mama with an iron fist. She was with him about eight years. Mama finally left him for good in 1995 and she moved back in with Mawmaw at our home place on the hill.

Several years after Mama left his mean ass he overdosed on Ativan. I was glad he was no longer on the planet to hurt anyone else. Who meets their future common law husband in a mental institute? Regardless, he was one of the great loves of her life. Was there any hope for Mama?

Every time I see a woman
At the bus stop
I see my mama's face
Praying to God to protect her
And touch her with his grace
The poor, the desperate, is she hurt again
Hoping in this game of life
She can finally win.
She turns up her collar
To shield her from the wind
But the coat she is wearing
Will not protect her from her sins.

Chapter 21- Her Girls Fled

In 1988 Joye moved in with another family friend, who became a mother to her and she called her Madre. She finished high school even though she missed over a month and a half of her junior year due to her serious knee issue. In 1990, Madre became pregnant and decided to move to Atlanta to be around her family. Joye soon followed. Madre had a boy and Joye had a baby brother! She doted on him and helped raise him. He was and is the light of her life. His middle name is Taylor. Joye and I intentionally chose not to have kids. The cycle stopped with us. Period. We didn't want to mess up or disappoint any of our own children. Our gene pool was not ideal either.

I also left Rutherford County in the summer of 1990. I moved to Gastonia, NC to start a new life and hopefully figure out my own journey. My dear friend Denise Greene (Neicy) talked me into getting away from my old life and trying something new. What a wise and caring lady. She saw something in me and knew I needed help. She single handedly changed my life.

Both of Mama's girls had moved away. It wasn't too big of a deal initially but over the years it would take its toll on her. Not seeing her girls regularly would eventually literally drive Mama madder. Joye and me both stayed in contact with Mawmaw and visited her regularly but Mama wasn't very involved with us. She was an energy thief. We loved her but we both realized we had to love her from arm's length so we could save ourselves.

Chapter 22- Back to Small Town Friendly

Mama had moved back to the homeplace on the hill in 1995. She ran into her childhood best friend Patsy one day in town at Kmart. They had not seen each other in years. Patsy had been carrying around in her pocketbook that little strawberry Christmas ornament that Mama had given her long ago. Patsy gave it back to Mama and told her that she had it for 30 years and now she wanted Mama to have it for the next 30 years.

Several months later they ran into each other again. That time it was at Hickory Log BBQ. Patsy said she really needed to see Mama that day. Her mama was terminal and was at Hospice House. Her sister was also in ICU at the local hospital and was critical. It was a very difficult time for Patsy. When she saw Mama she fell into her arms and cried. Mama held her and just let her cry. She then took Patsy over to see Mawmaw Betty. Mawmaw wrapped her loving arms around her and held her. That was the hardest time of Patsy's life and there was Mama when Patsy needed her the most.

Not too long after that I took Mama (HH707119) to the emergency room at Rutherford Hospital. She was desperate and she needed to be admitted to the fifth floor aka the Psychiatric Unit. I overheard the ER doctor on duty referring to my Mama. He was telling a nurse that Mama was depressed and she was sitting upstairs in her room all day smoking cigarettes. I confronted him about his flippant and insensitive attitude. I ensured he knew she did not smoke and did not have an upstairs. He was just one more person that was insensitive to mental illness. He should have been the example of empathy but made fun of her instead. She was already obviously suicidal and wounded so why would a doctor verbally pick the scab off of her wound?

February 8, 1995

Today I called Mawmaw and she said Mama was trying to get back into Rutherford Hospital on the psych. ward (5th floor). Mawmaw said Mama was not doing well at all. There are no beds available at this time. Mama is on a waiting list to be admitted. If you are suicidal how can there not be another immediate option? I wonder why she does not get intensive therapy and get on an antidepressant. I guess for some people it is not that easy. I have trouble separating Mama being sick and my Mama being a loser or copping out. I love her but I feel nothing maternal towards her. Mostly what I feel is pity.

February 9, 1995

I called Mawmaw and Mama was there. Mama does not sound too good. Mawmaw says she can't see how Mama can lay on the couch day after day. My Mama really needs intensive help. I don't think she is crazy but I think she suffers from major depression and cannot function. What kind of help does she need? Is it an inner struggle to work at it and fight daily to conquer this debilitating sickness? Will she ever change or will she die a poor lonely old woman with absolutely nothing? She drives Mawmaw nuts. Mawmaw always tries to protect her and somehow she finds it within herself to give Mama the benefit of the doubt time and time again. Mostly I find that Mawmaw just makes excuses for Mama and enables her.

I don't feel like I had a mother. The only protector I know is my Mawmaw. She loves me so much and sometimes Mama shows her jealousy. Mama used to take out her frustrations on me. I believed until I was in my late teens that I was really really bad. Everything was my fault. Nothing I did was good enough. She would tell me that on a regular basis that I was the reason that her life was so screwed up. If it was not for me she could have married so and so. In my eyes I was the root of all evil. I was lazy and worthless and I would NEVER be anything-EVER! She told me repeatedly that I would never amount to anything.

I know now that I am beautiful and different but a cloud shadows me. I hear an echo telling me that I cannot quite reach whatever it is I am striving for. I am not as good as the other girls. No matter what I accomplish it does not seem quite good enough. I fall short.

February 22, 1995

I talked to Mama last night. She seemed pretty good. She is working forty hours a week again at KMART. She says she might come down one night this week. I want her to see my pretty, freshly painted and clean house. I am proud of it. I love my Mama but she is not a Mama.

Myself the Muse

Help me now to myself I cried.
One last day and one last try.
I feel so weak and oh so pale.
My soul is screaming. Hear it wail.
The little girl, a ghost of time.
I just fell back into my mind.
My sword is drawn on the blackness of life.
Slashing at the days of strife.
Fighting harder with every breath.
Cherishing life.
Refusing death.

February 27, 1995

I am afraid to get angry because I don't want to upset whoever I am mad at. I am afraid they will leave me if I piss them off. One of my fears is that whoever loves me will leave me. It is not a normal fear but it is a genuine fear.I think that my biggest problem of all is feeling that I am unworthy and therefore deserve to be left. I never knew from day to day whether or not Mama would come home again. If she didn't what would my sister and I do? How would I take care of her? She was little and deserved so much more. I did too but I just didn't know it then.

Why do I feel almost as if it happened to some other child and maybe I watched it or knew about it? It almost doesn't seem real.

Mama made me feel terrible by accusing me of being ashamed of her because she was overweight. That was never the case. I was not ashamed of her, ever. I felt bad for her because she thought I was ashamed of her.

Our electricity was turned off many times and food was scarce. The fuel oil would run out in the winter time and we would be cold sometimes. We always found a way to get through it though. Mawmaw, Uncle Vernon, Church, or Crisis Intervention would come to our rescue. We worried about bills all the time and hoped life would improve.

Sometimes I feel an overwhelming loneliness and emptiness. When this occurs it is usually inexplicable. I am usually reaching for something in someone else but I never find it. I am very lonely. Today I am exceptionally lonely. I cannot seem to fill the emptiness today. I don't know how to stop it. I cannot stop it.

Why did you not hold me? Why must I always be the one to hold everyone else? The cycle stops here dammit. I am not going to let them make me crazy anymore. You with your pitiful tears and your venom tongue. Why won't you keep a job? Why must you depend on other people to pick you up? Why are you so damned lazy? Why do you not pay your bills? Why do you request-no demand pity from all those you touch? Why do you not take responsibility for me and free me from these crippling chains? Mawmaw should be enjoying these last years of her life instead of taking care of you. We have all enabled you your entire life. How many chances do you need or deserve? Why did you let our house get so nasty? Why did you let all the animals shit everywhere? Why did we have to have so many animals? Why did you have to beat me so much? Why did you slap me so many times? To humiliate me? To make yourself feel better? Well look at me now! I do not need you! What I do need from you is to quit needing us so much! I made me who I am-ME! My morals, dreams, ambitions, decency, my will to be everything I can, and my desire to help the less fortunate I made. These things came from my soul and my guts. I never had anyone to hold me and let me cry. There was never anyone to tell me everything is going to be all right. But I sure told you didn't I? Me and my ten year old little self with all the answers. It will be all right Mama.

I was born in '66
War abroad and war at home
She was sixteen and daddy was long gone
The house was full of lies
And the stench was in the air
Right from the beginning
They made a lovely pair
They left me here and there
Fast cars and women
Whiskey, gin, and booze
Choose between me and them
I would always lose
Mama ran off with anyone
Who gave her a second look
A desperate plea to let her
Off the mothering hook

Chapter 23- Hawg Heaven

On May 28, 1999 Mama turned 50. We surprised her by having her ride on a Harley during a bike event. She rode with George. He had long gray hair and a long gray braided beard. His bike was the lead bike on the twenty mile ride. Mama had a blast! I followed on my Harley and Joye rode with my dear friend Donna Meredith on her Harley. We finished the ride in York, SC at a cool bar that had an outdoor area. We had birthday cake, drinks, and all the fixins. Me, Mama, Mawmaw, and Joye danced and had a ball. Mawmaw had her Harley gear on too. We were all dancing, cuttin' up and having a great time celebrating Mama's milestone birthday. My crazy and fun loving girls were always receptive to try something different and fun. Many of the HOG Chapter members of Gastonia, NC, joined in on the birthday celebration. We made Mama's 50th birthday memorable for her.

Chapter 24- Crazier Than the Last Crazy Maker

She met her third husband at the local Moose Lodge. On April 1, 2001 Mama married him. He was 31 years old and Mama was 51. He was three years younger than me.

Mama The Muse July 19, 2001

Mama,

I am 34/35/36/37/38 years old and this never goes away. Here are a couple of things I want you to think about. Please take this to heart. Would you approve of me dating or marrying this guy? What would you do if you knew me, Joye, or Mawmaw was in an explosive and volatile relationship? You are after all someone's daughter and mother. Imagine driving down the road and suddenly you wonder at that very moment if your mother is okay. Every time the phone rings it makes your stomach hurt because you hope no one is calling to tell you bad news about your Mama again. Don't go back Mama. I love you. Robbie

Summer 2001

It is her choice to go back. She was away for a couple of months. She says she loves him. She says she misses him. She says she would rather die slowly with him than die slowly without him. Oh the wonders of mental illness and zero self-esteem.

This is her third unhealthy relationship. How many times is she going to put herself and her family through this? She lost her children largely due to this bewildering desire of hers to be in volatile relationships. Maybe she wants to be punished. I think her mind does that enough for her all ready. Grandma lets her control her. They feed off of one another. God help us all.

November 28, 2001 Slow Suicide

Mawmaw has not heard from her. Something is wrong as usual. Probably will not be a Christmas. If Mawmaw has to buy the presents for Mama to give away then there will not be any gifts this year. Fine by me. I am not buying anything anymore. I am done…done…done.

Mawmaw hurt her ankle and needs Mama's help, but doesn't get it. Slow suicide. I cannot dwell on it and worry. I cannot think about her lifelong misery……………until the next tragedy.

November 29, 2001   I'll Be Leaving You Always

Left you at fourteen but I never got away. I left my little sister in the path of your misery. I live with that every day. You left me at two years and six months old. You live with that every day. From the cradle to the grave I was taught that your love has conditions. Your demons you fought. I hate you, go to hell you screamed. Your shouts of choice. I was a sad child. I had no voice. How did I get myself into this you cried. Help me find a way out you pleaded. How could a twelve year old little girl help you Mama? There was always a cloud of doubt, wondering why you do not or cannot love me or maybe you just do not know how. Time has a way of hunting you down and that is why you wear your eternal frown.

November 31, 2001   9:40 PM

Miserable skin needs miserable pain. She picked him up yesterday morning. She has a car. He does not. He does not work. She draws disability. Now she pops pills and drinks a lot.

My neighbor came over yesterday morning at 1:00 a.m. to use the phone to call 911. it just so happened that my Mama was scheduled to represent herself in court. I do not know the outcome. Anyway, neighbor woman left in handcuffs in the back of a cop car. I do not know if her husband was arrested. She was yelling apologies to her six year old son. He was hysterically crying for his mama.

So now we will count the days until it happens again. I think this is about the third time she has gone back to him and they have been together about six months including three of those as man and wife. Yes. She married his mean ass. I hope she is safe. She will go to the hospital (mental or medical) again. She will leave him again and hopefully this time she will stay away. I am highly concerned for her safety.

What a selfish and humorous woman she is. It is so bizarre it is comical. Nothing matters. No reasoning. It makes no sense at all. She does not need him financially. There are no young children involved. She is addicted to drama. There is no other way. Just hysteria and fit pitching and driving Mawmaw crazy. It is making me anxious yet again. I am numb I think. I catch myself shaking my head and sighing heavily.

December 1, 2001

The men came and went over the years but before they would go there was always some desperation from you. You were searching. You are searching. What are you looking for? It was something your two little girls obviously could not give you. We had no voice. We had no food. We had no money. We had no electricity. We had no nurturing. We had no lunch money. We had nothing strong in our house except the stench of dirty dishes, dirty clothes, and animal shit. I wonder if we stunk. When you did sweep you swept it out of the back door of our ratty ass trailer into our nasty back yard. We had clothes piled to the ceiling and cats shit in our corners. We did get free lunch though. Free lunch kids. I always thought free lunch kids belonged in special education classes. God got mad. I always felt that was the reason why our trailer burned down. It was too nasty to continue living in. I do not know why our next one was nasty though. I meant to wash the dishes better. I meant to wash them all before they were used again. You always chose the man over your girls. Your baby girl adored you. You put her through hell. No one like you Mama. I watched her heart break and spill onto the floor. I held her ten year old body to my fourteen year old body when she cried for you. She hated me for it. She hated me for not being you. When you ran off with your first abuser she came to live with me at Daddy's. I guess you could not take being a mother anymore. You always told me that I would come home from school one day and you would be gone. I was the root of all evil. I was the reason for your fucked up life. "If it hadn't been for you Robbie" Guess you would have been a brain surgeon if it had not been for me.

December 1, 2001 Still

Still no word from Mama. Mawmaw is used to hearing from her daily. Mama's friend went by today to see her. She said she looked fine. Mama is going to church. I hope it helps. Good luck and a band aid. You're gonna need it.

December 10, 2001 Invite him for ham?

Mawmaw thinks we should consider inviting him to my house for Christmas dinner. I have never met him nor do I want to. I need to talk to my sister. I do not want him at my house. I do not want to see him. I doubt Mama shows up anyway.

December 11, 2001 Permission denied

Mawmaw needed Mama to take her to the doctor. She called Mama and Mama said she would have to ask permission. She actually said that out loud. Mama called Mawmaw back and told her it would be best to get someone else to take her. I guess that takes care of the decision about inviting him to Christmas dinner or not. Hell no! No ham for him. I never met him and neither did Joye and I am not sorry about that.

December 12, 2001 Coward

I found out that Mama did not ask about taking Mawmaw to the doctor. I guess she just did not want to deal with it. I do not know if she will show up for Christmas dinner.

December 22, 2001 Silent Night

We had our Christmas dinner at my new house. Mama showed up very late and very fucked up. She was in bad shape. Downers. She said she had popped a Xanex before she came. I think she meant to say several Xanex. He did not show. She had a new video camera that she could not afford. She rewound and retaped anything that was said that she thought might cause her any issues. It was sad.

January 1, 2002 Out With The Old

Happy New Years. Mawmaw said Mama left him again. There had been an altercation that resulted in 911 being called, the police coming, Mama's wrists being cut, and him being arrested for resisting arrest and he pled guilty. I told a friend about it. She said the weirdest part of the story was how mundane I made it sound. She said I spoke as casually as if I were asking for someone to pass the salt.

January 2, 2002 5th Floor?

I called Mawmaw and Mama was visiting and answered the phone. She is staying with a friend and she said she needed to talk to me. She is thinking of going into the hospital again. I wonder how many times she has been hospitalized for tragedies now.

January 16, 2002 Wrist Slashing

Mama is in the hospital psych. unit again. This time she is in Kings Mountain Hospital where she is getting Electroconvulsive Therapy (ECT shock therapy) treatments again. She is barely hanging on. I do the obligatory good daughter visits. Her friend told Mawmaw that Mama cut her own wrists.

January 17, 2002 PSYCH

I went to see Mama last night. She seems to be all right. At least I know she is safe for a few days. She confessed to me that she did cut her own wrists and showed me where. I did not want to see her latest trophy. I had to turn away.

Chapter 25- Still Trying to Die

When Mawmaw Betty's mama (Bernice Honeycutt) passed away she left her little trailer to Mawmaw Betty. It was old and needed some work but Mawmaw wanted to move it beside the homeplace on the hill. She wanted to ensure that Mama had her own place to live. It cost about a thousand dollars to have it moved and set up. The move cost way more than the trailer was worth but it was important to Mawmaw to continue to try and save Mama. She moved in and out of the trailer. Most of the time her best friend would live with her.

Mama had significant conflict resolution issues. What might be perceived as a simple situation to resolve was often too stressful for Mama to deal with in a healthy manner. She struggled to stand up for herself. It was all consuming and impossible to face head on. Her best friend who was also her roommate at the time was supposed to move out of Mama's trailer but changed her mind and did not leave. Mama could not stand confrontation, so instead of asking or making her friend leave, she reached her breaking point and attempted suicide again.

On January 12, 2004 she (H707119) was admitted through the ER to the fifth floor Psychiatric Unit again. While there she was not very cooperative in her treatment. She operated on her own schedule, was disruptive at times, and did not participate appropriately in the programs. Her affect was downcast and constricted. Her presentation was hopeless. Mama told one of the nurses that she would overdose again but denied saying that to her doctor. So it was determined that she was no longer a threat to herself and she was to go back to outpatient group therapy twice a week. She had reached the maximum benefit from hospitalization and was discharged from the hospital on January 16, 2004. It was determined that within four days she went from suicidal to no longer a threat to herself or others.

That same evening she (H707119) was admitted to Rutherford Hospital Fifth floor again. She tried to commit suicide once again by overdosing. She had lined her medications up on a bench. Her friend came in and found her unconscious. She called 911 and Mama was rushed to the ER for a serious overdose. That time she was in ICU unit ICU02-A until January 19, 2004. Fortunately she was able to make a full physical recovery. Unfortunately she said her life sucks and she does not want to be here. She said if she can get a bottle of pills she will take them again. Joye still lived in Atlanta and I had moved to Indianapolis in 2003. Moving to Indy was one of the best decisions I ever made and it was one of the best things that ever happened to me. I happened to be home that weekend visiting when Mama took the pills.

When Mama was released again on January 19, 2004 me and Joye had her moved to Spartanburg Hospital. We needed to protect her from herself so we had her transferred again. On January 21, 2004 we had her involuntarily committed to Charter Hospital of Greenville, SC by the police. That was also known as Carolina's Center For Behavioral Health. There are no records on file due to them being destroyed. In SC, medical records can legally be destroyed after ten years.

On October 16, 2004 Mama was stressed again about her same old best friend moving back in with her. Mama struggled to set limits and had constant suicidal thoughts. She was sad, depressed, helpless, and felt hopeless. She didn't attempt suicide but contacted Mawmaw to come next door and get her. Knowing Mama's history, Mawmaw took her to the ER and she was admitted to the fifth floor Psychiatric Unit again. Mama was placed on a 15 minute watch due to her then recent serious suicide attempt. Mama's effect was sad, and her mood was depressed. She stated that her life was not worth living. There was stress in her home that she could not confront or cope with. On October 23, 2004 Mama stated that she hoped to have a more realistic viewpoint about taking on the burdens of others. Ultimately she was deemed to no longer be a threat to herself and she was released on October 25, 2004. So in one week she was repaired?

She went back to the outpatient programs that she had been in and out of for at least 10 years (Insights, Family Preservation, and New Vista). None of them were successful. She struggled to show up on time if at all. The reality was that she could barely get off the couch and often did not go out of the house for weeks at a time.

Chapter 26- Hoarding

As Mawmaw got older she accumulated more "stuff". Each time someone she was close to passed away she would get some of their "stuff". It became more and more difficult to manage. She was also born and raised during the Great Depression and she didn't like to waste anything. She meant well and tried to recycle. As she aged it became impossible for her to accomplish yet she continued to try. Mama moved back in with Mawmaw in 1995. Mama became fully disabled in 1998 and stayed home with Mawmaw. Together they accumulated, collected, and acquired more than they could control.

On two different occasions I called a company to inquire about the cost of cleaning out the homeplace on the hill. They would come in and clean out the house end to end for $3,000.00. I wouldn't be able to go through and salvage anything if I did that. There were a few things that meant a lot to me and I wanted to keep family pictures, Mawmaw's old cookbooks, Mawmaw Bernice's apron, and a few other keepsakes. So over the last eight years I rented a commercial dumpster and cleaned out approximately five tons of "stuff". I had it hauled off from our homeplace on the hill. It was approximately a thousand dollars each time and there were four times.

Chapter 27- Mawmaw Betty

Mawmaw and her second husband remained married even though they were separated. They had somewhat of a long distance relationship. Mawmaw left him in 1985 and moved back to the homeplace on the hill. She left him for several reasons and one of them was because he couldn't take all the drama that came with Mawmaw's baggage AKA Mama. He told Mawmaw to leave one time too many and so she did. Guess that runs in the family.

He passed away in September of 2007. I was living in out of state at that time and I flew home to be with Mawmaw and our family. In addition, I had previously planned to come the next weekend and I still did. I spent that day with Daddy at the fall festival in downtown Rutherfordton. We had a sweet time hanging out together. That evening I took Mama and Mawmaw to Walmart to loaf (southern term for browse). Mawmaw got stuff to make me breakfast the next morning. It was mine and Mawmaw's tradition. Every time I went home she would cook my favorite breakfast. Being the phenomenal southern cook she was, I could not wait to enjoy her feast. She would make her special biscuits from scratch and homemade Mawmaw style gravy. Homemade jam was plentiful and added an extra layer of love because she had made it herself. Eggs scrambled hard and fried livermush (southern breakfast food and I'll leave it at that) topped off my treat. The best part of the meal was knowing that it was made with her weathered and arthritic hands. Hands that picked thick and endless rows of cotton since she was 5 years old. Hands that hauled water from the creek to the house because they didn't have running water when she was growing up. Hands that made clothing that many of us in her family wore. Hands that used feed sacks or cottonseed sacks to make dresses for her family. Oh how those hands loved me!

But God had other plans for our matriarch. She got very sick that night. She tried to get out of bed to go to the bathroom. I grabbed her as she started to stumble. We gently fell down onto the bed. I held her in my arms against me. We had to call 911 to take her to the ER at the local hospital. We were there all night and since they confirmed that she didn't have a heart attack they sent her home. Without fail, she would always stand on the front porch and watch me drive away. We would wave and blow each other kisses until each of us faded out of sight. I left on Sunday evening to go back home. I knew Mawmaw didn't feel good because she didn't walk me to the door like she did every single time I had ever left her home dating back to September of 1966. However, I did sit in her lap before I left. I was 41 years old and one of my favorite things in life was to sit on my Mawmaw's lap.

Two days later I got a phone call from Mama. Mawmaw was having a massive heart attack. Just like that she was gone. Our matriarch and my first love was gone. The rock of our family and our lifeline had crossed the river. Wow! The planet looked different and the whole world hurt. Life couldn't possibly continue to happen with Mawmaw not there. I never got to enjoy that breakfast we had planned. The food I had bought remained in the freezer for many years until I eventually cleaned it out.

I came right back to the homeplace on the hill that night. We were all devastated. I was broken to my bones. I stayed with Mama for two weeks trying to tidy up Mawmaw's affairs and be with Mama. Responsible adult life called and I had to get back to work. I had to go.

I left Mama alone in the house without Mawmaw. The same homeplace on the hill that both of her parents died in. I remember heading down the driveway and watching Mama as I drove away. I didn't know how or if Mama would make it without Mawmaw. She would go on to spend days, weeks, months, and even years on the couch in our homeplace on the hill. No cleaning occurred, no visitor's much, and no going out much. Her life was tortured. Her kids were gone and now her mama, best friend, enabler, nemesis, and love of her life was gone too. Her house fell apart around her. She began to disappear, almost dissolve into the darkness that was her life. The squalor overtook what used to be a home and Mama was getting swallowed by it.

What I failed to realize was that Mama lost her Mama. I lost my hero, moral compass, friend, grandmother, and favorite human but Mama lost her Mama! It would take me years but eventually I would come to understand how powerfully painful and life altering that was. Mama had earned her loneliness and isolation like a soldier's medal. Her self- imposed misery was evident. I revered Mawmaw and would have given her the moon. I was always there for Mama and I loved her unconditionally but my love for her was more guarded. Impending doom and lack of hope were constant emotions I carried around towards her. She was envious of mine and Joye's relationship with Mawmaw. Perhaps subconsciously I was punishing Mama somehow for all the times she had let us down. I adored Mawmaw and I let the whole world know it. Mama was remarkably grateful to Mawmaw for taking care of us but she longed for her own special relationship with her girls. Mama literally was alone. She was aging and there were no men around anymore. Her friends were scarce and her physical health was changing. Her guts now screamed for her children and she still needed to be saved. Mama was powerfully stressful to be around. Her energy would suck the life out of you if you let it. She was blue, negative, and her house was unbearable to go into.

Mama rarely went anywhere. Aunt Joy, Aunt Gail, and Uncle Bill would call her regularly and ask her to go to a ball game, go to the fish camp (southern term for seafood restaurant) or come over to their houses and eat. They all lived within a couple of miles of each other. Mama wanted to go but she could barely even bathe herself anymore much less go out. She loved her family and thought of her little cousins as her nieces and nephews. Mama would have given her left arm to have been able to go see them play ball or cheerlead. Instead she spent most of her time and life at home alone. She was low and barely functioning. Every single day was a struggle for her. Joye and me lived out of town and didn't visit very often and Mama was consumed with guilt. It was the type of deep and powerful guilt that comes from being a not so good mother. She could barely live with herself and she detested herself for it. She was paying a price on a debt she had very little control over. She was truly a tortured soul. Her agony was all consuming and that made it even more difficult to be around her. She seemed to digress when Joye and me were around her or talking to her. She would often talk to us as if we were small children. She would even sign her greeting cards "Love, Mommy". I think she wished she could do it all over again so she pretended we were still little kids. That felt awkward to me but I never said anything to her about it. As an adult I avoided hurting her feelings at all cost.

She had developed some health problems that were added on top of her mental health issues. She had arthritis, a bad back, irritable bowel syndrome, and asthma. I worked through a local mental health agency and got her an assistant to help her with a few things such as running errands and light housekeeping. The assistants helped her finally get her divorce from her third husband. However, there were some issues with the assistants. It seemed they struggled to show up on time or at all. The mental health system was and still is underfunded and the pay for that position was low. That made it a challenge to get quality people. Mama decided not to use their help anymore because they were unreliable and unreliability added additional irrational stress to her life.

Mama was also starting to have significant problems with her teeth. It was eventually confirmed that she would need to have them pulled. She later told me that was the most devastating thing that had ever happened to her. The vast amount of medicines she took over most of her adult life were unkind to her teeth as were her abusive relationships.

Countless times I considered taking over her care. I was advised by a close friend to leave the government out of it because once that door is opened it cannot be undone. I did ask Mama several times if she wanted me to manage her money for her. She considered it but decided to continue to manage her own money. She struggled mightily in that area and failed often. I don't think Mama ever understood that being on full disability would limit her options when it came to housing and medical treatment. She didn't have to pay any rent because Mawmaw's house was paid for which was a huge blessing. However, having no rent to pay caused her to only get $36.00 a month in food stamps. Years ago Mawmaw and I went to a lawyer. She had a right to life drawn up so that the moment she passed I would be the sole owner of the homeplace. She did that to ensure Mama always had a place to live. She knew Mama was incapable of managing the upkeep on the house. She also knew I would pay the taxes, insurance, upkeep, and ensure Mama stayed warm in the winter.

Chapter 28- Inpatient/Outpatient

As part of Mama's outpatient program she was supposed to meet with her psychiatrist once a month to do a medication management program and have in home visits from her caseworker. Her psychiatrist was concerned that Mama was not managing her medicine correctly. He suggested that she be placed in a supervised environment where group counseling was required. She was admitted to the psychiatric ward on the fifth floor again.

Her affect was wide ranging and she tried to convince the interviewer of her normalcy. She lives in seclusion and does not answer her phone. She is pleasant, cooperative and has no mania at this time. She was released after a few days when the doctor was confident that her medications were under control.

On December 12, 2008 when Mama was 59 years old she met with her caseworker. She had significant unresolved grief over losing Mawmaw. She had lost 60 pounds, had poor impulse control, and was spending her small $600.00 monthly income unwisely. She had maxed out several credit cards and was spending uncontrollably. At that time anyone could get credit cards, even people on disability. Her caseworker stated that Mama's house was a filthy environment and that she was possibly in a hoarding situation. Her speech was slow and her hygiene was fair. She appeared disheveled, her affect was flat, and her intelligence level appeared average. Mama told the caseworker "I kinda gave up on me." Hope was a thing of the past.

On January 5, 2009 Mama had another medicine management meeting. Her drug screen showed negative for Ritalin. She explained that she was out of money for it but would not elaborate as to why. She was anxious and preoccupied but not suicidal.

On May 28, 2009 Mama's medicine management meeting was on her 60th birthday. She was more optimistic than the last visit. She showed her doctor pictures of her cat and her three dogs that she was very proud of. She went to counseling twice a week.

On June 29, 2009 Mama was discharged from outpatient treatment due to compliance issues with attendance and medication management. She was depressed, hopeless and helpless, and still had unresolved grief. Her anxiety, guilt, shame, and poor decision making were overwhelming to her. She was told she could return to outpatient therapy when she was able to commit to therapy and medication management. Her therapist stated that she might benefit from community support and she should consider doing some volunteer work. Wow! Now that is a great idea but she can barely get off the couch. Really?

Chapter 29- Round Two

In the fall of 2011 Mama texted me and asked me to call her. She told me she had been seeing the guy that was her boyfriend back in 1979 again. It was bad back then. What could he possibly want from her this time? I was highly leery but she wanted me to give him another chance. On the inside the child in me was screaming no I still hate him but in reality I had forgiven him many years ago. He was one of the reasons I had left my Mama's home back in 1981. I left my little sister there and that was a decision I would regret to this day. I knew Mama wanted company and she was lonely. I told her I would proceed with caution and that I wanted her to be happy more than anything. She told me he had changed. He would have to prove it for me to believe it.

She left our homeplace on the hill and moved to Charlotte to live with him. He didn't have a car but he did at least have a job at that time. Even though she enjoyed the city, it was not too long until she was calling me to come and get her.

I drove to Charlotte and took her to Zoe's Kitchen for lunch. We sat outside and enjoyed the uptown city view and skyline. It's funny looking back. I had never seen, stood, hugged, or spent any time with her except in Rutherford County, NC, Columbia, SC, a few times, and of course her beloved Myrtle Beach. She showed me her favorite building. She also told me things were not too good. I knew pretty quickly that it wasn't what she had hoped it would be but she decided to stay with him anyway. They moved into a nicer apartment and enjoyed their new neighbors and things seemed better. Mama was very friendly and loved people. But shortly after that he lost his job. They quickly got evicted and Mama moved back to our homeplace on the hill. He followed her.

She told me she didn't want him there but she still had those same old confrontation issues. Her conflict management skills had not improved and were almost nonexistent. The homeplace on the hill needed some repairs and a lot of cleaning. Since he didn't work he was supposed to help take care of the house but that didn't really happen. They were living off of Mama's SSI (social security income) and disability. That was a total of $720.00 a month. She could be easily manipulated and would give up control without much pushback. She gave up and became compliant. Conflict, controversy, and confrontation was still something she ran from and was irrational about.

Chapter 30- The Symptoms Were There

On June 6, 2013 Mama was not feeling well so she went to her general practitioner for a checkup. She felt sick all over, was having trouble swallowing food, and was having night sweats. Other symptoms were black stool and blood in the toilet. She was nauseous and had stomach pain. She couldn't have an upper scope to run tests due to the gastric bypass she had in 1981. She was sent home with what appeared to be irritable bowel syndrome. At that visit Mama was taking 12 medicines including: Abilify (depression), Cymbalta (depression), Neurontin (nerve pain), Adderall (ADHD), Celebrex (arthritis), Topamax (migraines), Toporal (angina), Zyrtec, Prilosec, Symbicort (asthma), Albuterol (asthma), and Flonase.

Chapter 31- Fifth Floor Again

On June 24, 2013 Mama (H707119) voluntarily committed herself into the Psychiatric Unit at Rutherford Hospital. She was out of control and hated being around her boyfriend. She was concerned that violence might occur between the two of them. During that visit she was diagnosed with diabetes. The 19 medications she was on at that time were: Wellbutrin (antidepressant), Buspar (anxiety), Atarax (muscle relaxer), Zanaflex (muscle relaxer), Trazadone (antidepressant), Geodon (bi-polar medication), Centrum, Vitamin C, Albuterol (asthma), Symbicort (asthma), Celebrex (arthritis), Zyrtec, Cymbalta (nerve pain/antidepressant), Flonase, Neurontin (nerve pain), Antivert (vertigo), Protonix, Topomax (migraines), Ventolin inhaler (asthma). Six of these medicines were to treat her mental illness.

The patient is a 64 year old female who was admitted as a direct admission from her psychiatrist's office where she presented with increasing depression and anxiety over the past week. Her boyfriend had apparently been more verbally abusive towards her and conflict increased. The patient was quite irritable, having wishes to be dead, and thoughts of overdosing (she knew the key words to say). She was initially placed on observations every 15 minutes. She eventually settled into the unit and participated well in group and milieu (social) therapies. Patient's mood continued to improve and she denied having any SI (self-injury), HI (homicidal ideation), AVH (auditory verbal hallucinations), or thoughts of self-harm. She also eventually denied having any problems with depression, anxiety, mood lability (mood swings), or irritability. Patient was subsequently placed on routine observations. Her mood continued to improve and eventually reached a euthymic state (normal non-depressed, reasonably positive mood). Patient denied any adverse medication side effects. The patient was subsequently discharged in good condition with full activity and a regular diet with the following discharge diagnoses:

AXIS I: Major depression, recurrent and severe, improved. Anxiety disorder, unspecified. Obstructive sleep apnea, improved.

AXIS II: Personality disorder unspecified.

AXIS III: Asthma, arthritis.

AXIS IV: Moderate to severe psychosocial stressors.

AXIS V: GAF upon assessment 20.

She would later tell me that looking back the sickness came to her while she was in the Psychiatric Unit (5th floor). She was eating lunch and all of a sudden she pushed her plate away. From that moment on her appetite was gone. She consistently struggled with her weight so not having an appetite was a blessing at the time. After eight days she was discharged from the hospital on July 2, 2013.

She couldn't take another minute of being with him. She told me that she despised him and was fearful violence might occur. She ended up going back to our homeplace on the hill and of course he was still there. She was miserable and she told me she didn't love him.

He would get upset with her if she didn't do what he thought she ought to. He was jealous of me and Joye. However, he would call me and try to get me to help him or talk to her for him. It was highly evident he had temper control issues. I could usually calm him down and I could tell in his voice and breathing when he was struggling to keep his composure. I got tired of those calls but selfishly I was glad he was there to at least be with Mama. I knew in my heart things weren't right. Selfishly I was thankful she had someone around all the time in case she fell or got hurt. I didn't know the extent of the abuse. Should I have known? Should I have acted?

When she was single, all she did was sleep. She rarely went anywhere and would spend days and sometimes weeks at home alone. She was withdrawn and I saw a change in her social skills. At least when she was with him they would often go places like the Goodwill store or flea markets. It was nice to see her out and about and sometimes she seemed less miserable.

Chapter 32- How Do I Tell Her

In 2009, Daddy was diagnosed with COPD (chronic pulmonary obstructive disease) and had considerable issues with his health. He was in and out of ICU multiple times and we almost lost him a time or two. Mama asked about him often. Daddy would ask about her too. He would say to me, "I rode by your Mama's house and her car ain't been there in 3 days. Is she alright?" Daddy continued to be in and out of the hospital until he died suddenly from a massive heart attack on September 21, 2013. It was a surprise but not a shock due to the seriousness of his COPD. It was hard to believe Daddy was gone though. Telling Joye was hard and I struggled to figure out how to tell Mama. I knew it would send her reeling. I was right.

She came to Daddy's service and when we all went outside to see the full military honors and the doves being released, Mama hugged me from behind. She was clinging to me for dear life and literally hanging on me. It was a physical strain. In my head I was thinking calm down Mama because this is Daddy's day. I would never hurt her feelings like that but I thought it. She looked beautiful in her black dress. She had been losing weight and looked fantastic. Little did I know as my Mama stood holding on to me as we laid Daddy to rest, she had a killer manifesting inside of her. There was a mighty storm brewing that no one knew about and only God could heal.

Section 3: The Sickness, The Beacon

Chapter 33- The Beach One Last Time

Twenty days after daddy died, on October 11, 2013 Mama and her boyfriend were going to Myrtle Beach. She wanted to come by and see me since my house was on the way to the beach. When they pulled up and Mama opened the car door, I knew immediately something was very wrong. When she stepped out of the car I asked her what was going on. She was highly jaundiced. She said it started a few days prior but she felt ok. I was immediately alarmed. I knew in my heart something was awfully wrong. Oddly enough she hadn't mentioned to me how bad she felt prior to her arrival. Mama's physical health had started to deteriorate a smidge (southern term for a bit). She had the mental health shuffle (her long term overmedicated gait was shuffle like) but she was weaker and noticeably more frail than usual. The Internet is a cruel truth teller. When she left my instinct was that she was very, very sick. I talked her into going straight to the ER at Myrtle Beach. I drove down to the beach the next morning to be with her. Tests were ran and within a day the doctors were fairly certain she had cancer. She stayed in the hospital at Myrtle Beach for a few days for more tests. From there she would be transferred to Charlotte, NC.

Before she left for Charlotte she wanted to see the ocean. So on the night before she had to leave she decided to check out of the hospital and check into her hotel. The Admiral on Ocean Blvd at the 2nd Avenue Pier at Myrtle Beach (her favorite place) gave her an oceanfront room since she didn't get there to honor her reservations of a few days prior. She had pizza for supper and slept with the sliding door open so she could hear the ocean. "It was in the fall in the autumn of her life when she learned it was really her late winter and she would likely lose her life in the spring. She asked not of her material possessions but asked only who will take care of her two greatest assets......her daughters."

On Wednesday Oct. 13, 2013, Mama went to Novant Presbyterian Hospital in Charlotte. Mama and I agreed that she should go there. It was closer to our family and the hospital had a good reputation. My childhood best friend, Susan Metcalf Barnhart, worked there and I knew she would ensure Mama was taken care of. More tests were done in Charlotte. A biliary drain tube was placed into her side that allowed her pancreas to drain. The hope was that the drain tube would alleviate the jaundice. Mama stayed in the hospital a few days. We feared the worst and the tests revealed that the head of the pancreas had a 2.3 cm. tumor in it. She was sent home while they waited on additional test results. In the meantime the drain tube gave her some problems. As it turned out the biliary tube had caused an infection. The hospital unfortunately never gave any instructions or cleaning materials for her to take home. She ended up back in the hospital. It was a pretty serious infection and it was uncomfortable to her. She didn't complain but if asked she would reveal.

On October 15, 2013 she had an oncology appointment back in Charlotte. The Doctor told us the tumor was inoperable and the outlook was dire. It was inoperable because of the location of the tumor and the gastric bypass she had in 1981. Her weight issues and that gastric bypass hounded her all of her adult life. I think we all knew that but hearing it out loud was a challenge. Joye was on speakerphone and asked the doctor some questions. He told us the average person lives six months after diagnosis. Pancreatic cancer has one of the lowest survival rates of all cancers.

When the doctor left the room to make arrangements for a local oncology visit, Mama put her head on my shoulder and asked me, "What have I ever done to deserve this?" I held on to her and told her that it had nothing to do with her. It was a dormant demon that finally manifested itself. No one in our family had ever had pancreatic cancer. That was the only time Mama even came near complaining. I asked her if she was scared and she said no. I told her I wouldn't be scared either then. She said, "Baby I can see it on your face." Mama was sad for Joye and me because our Daddy had just passed away suddenly 20 days prior to her official diagnosis. She didn't think it was fair for us to lose both of our young parents so close together. Mama took Daddy's passing hard and she wasn't happy her grieving daughters would now be losing their Mama as well. She was starting to show signs of selflessness.

Chapter 34- Blessings in the Pain

I was petrified down to my DNA. I had researched the best oncologists in the state and luckily one of the top doctors practiced in our hometown, Forest City, NC. What a surprising blessing. Her options were to do nothing, try chemo treatments, or see if there were any clinical trials available. Unfortunately, no clinical trials were available in our area that was a fit for Mama. She wanted to stay as close to home as possible so her family could visit her. The plan was to have eight chemotherapy treatments to hopefully slow the growth of the tumor and prolong its spreading to other places in her body. Quietly some of us thought she might roll over and tap out. History is a great predictor for the future. But surprisingly she wanted to fight.

Her first treatment went as well as could be expected. She had significant nausea and couldn't eat. Her weight changed quickly. We were unbelievably blessed that such a highly regarded oncologist had agreed to see her. He was one of the best in the state and was based in our county. It also helped that our sweet cousin Denita Vickers used to work for him and was a patient of his during her own battle with breast cancer.

Oct. 13 jaundice-admitted to MB

Oct. 15 CLT-well nourished

Our Daddy passed on Sept 21, 2013. Three weeks later Mama was diagnosed with terminal pancreatic cancer. It's interesting how life works out sometimes. On the day of Mama's official diagnosis I was notified that Daddy had left me and Joye some money. I was told which bank to go to and I had no idea how much money he had left us. The teller told me Daddy had left each of us $2,700.00 dollars. I was so grateful that he thought to leave us some of his life's earnings. As it turned out I got twenty seven one hundred dollar bills. I'm not sure why but when I got home I put it in tin foil and placed it in the freezer. Looking back that sounds like something quirky Daddy would have done. As Mama's new cancer journey progressed I went to visit her more. Each time I went I took money from the freezer. Eventually I would take a hundred dollar bill each time I went. I bought her anything she needed or wanted. She never asked for anything but if prodded she would tell me what food she was craving. As it turned out Daddy helped me take care of Mama in her final days and he never knew it. I told Mama about it and it delighted her to know that his money was helping her. Mama's SSI and disability checks went straight to her medical bills. Daddy's money aka freezer money was pivotal in helping us. Thanks Dink!

Mama The Muse

Oct. 30, 2013 she weighed 182.

Nov. 5, 2013 11 meds.

Nov. 8, 2013 she weighed 184.6 pounds. Awesome oncologist and gemzar chemo drug. 16 meds. Nov. 11, 2013 she weighed 184 lbs. with her coat on at Dr's. office.

Nov. 13, 2013 she weighed 183.6. and 23 meds.

Nov. 15, 2013 I was tied to her for life. Her eyes are green and mine are too. She gave my daddy one then # two.

November 20, 2013.

 Parking Level 2 Yellow. Charlotte again. She had to have her biliary tube replaced and infection fought.

 My eyes are hot and my cheek is wet.
 Praying to God that I do not forget.
 Praying to God no regrets.
 Her voice it shook and her words they froze.
 Her eyes welled up and I reached for her hand.
 And the same words I have said a thousand times rolled off my tongue.
 Don't cry mama.
 It's gonna be all right mama.
 She had taken a shower and washed her hair.
 She was waiting for my arrival as if I was a rock star.
 And we walked.

Nov. 24, 2013

Thinking of her and Praying for her and my silent noise.
Physical therapy confirmed today.
Simple little things that make my day.
Fading like a flower.
I think I shall die in the fall.
I will be with the rest of yall.
I'll fly away with the autumn leaves.
And blow away in the evening breeze.
Like you and you and now it's you.   September and October-my
fav time of the year.   But it's different now because yall ain't
here.

Nov. 25, 2015

So here I am and there you are.
Miles between us but not that far.
Ties to you by blood and years.
In the battlefield to fight back the tears.

Nov. 26, 2013

Today was better and her voice more clear.
I am thanking the stars that she is still here.
In a blaze of glory and a flash of light.
She will disappear into the night.
Like a vapor or a mist or steam after the rain.
Hopping the rail on a north bound train.
Fading like a flower.
Now her feet don't work so how's she gonna dance?
We will groove with our eyes and get funky in our hearts.
Just Mama and daughter rocking in the dark.
The sun is setting high and autumn starts to give it up to the cold.
Winter is coming and she looks so old.
Demons from her past are going to fly away like blackbirds.
No depression on high and no lows.
The king of king's will take her pain and drag it away like demons to be put to rest
and we shall be left behind and put to the test.
She will move on and live with joy.

Nov. 27, 2013

Full chemo.
PT in the works.
2 Mickey's dbl cheeseburgers,
still at 183 lbs, 8:00PM and she is asleep.
Chemo was hard on her.

Thanksgiving 2013

We knew this would be our last one together here on earth. I showed mama a current picture of
her, me, and Joye and she didn't recognize herself. She asked me who that was and when I told her
she softly replied, "no it's not." I didn't correct her.

Nov. 30, 2013

Do something fun today I said.
I walked to the living room and played with the cats.
I walked to the kitchen and ate a pear she said.

Dec 1, 2013

Rob enjoy.
Beef stew and rice she said.
Been thinking of her all day.
Chill in the air and an ache in my heart.

Dec 2, 2013

Hopeful. Anxious. Sad.Happy.

Jesus take control. Stupid eyes leaking again. Let us dull our tongues instead of speaking bitter hateful words no one deserves to hear. If you love me pick me up lift me skyward only one way up and up until the sky parts and I am whole again. This is a journey, no a safari that I must go on. Pain does not describe it. Agony does not describe it. There is a darkness and a light. There is a wrong and there is a right but right is just that. She came around in the spring of '49. My pain runs as deep as my bloodline beneath my skin. My little daddy. My mama cuz. I do not ask why. Fall has become my favorite dreaded season where all the old, weary, mad and worn are swept away like leaves from a driveway. Turning brilliant colors from gold to red to orange and more. Leaving in a quiet rush of wind until the ache of winter reminds me of my own arthritic back and hips. I am right behind them. Knocking on the door and clanging the gate. When will it be my turn to fly through the clouds and see my life givers? My eternal friends? I thought she would live another ten or fifteen years and die from a massive heart attack alone with her animals. Instead it sprung upon us like an unexpected teen pregnancy that was also her experience at 16. Who knew? It was dormant and lying in wait like a killer behind a tree with all its jaundice and voice altering drugs. Nausea and shaking hands. Unbalanced walking and a bedside potty. A godsend that potty but a frightening sight for this child to see it right beside my mama's bed where I once stood as an aching child on Christmas morning. Waiting to open toys and see what mama santa got us. Us yes us. Two girls. Trying to keep up and stay out of the way. Loved hard and hardly loved. Oh the pain that one person can impose. Oh the love that one person can give. The cotton is high now but you don't pick no more. I got your shoes in a box sitting by the door. Walking down the street or driving in my car. Everywhere I go there you are.

Dec. 3, 2013 When I arrived

ADMITTED ICU05

I stand here beside you Mama where you are fighting to live. In 2004, almost 20 years before in this very unit Mama I stood here beside you where you were fighting to die by your own hand.

Chapter 35- DNR Not Today

I was headed to be with Mama while she had chemo. I knew she had been having some issues with her blood pressure being low. When she got to the doctor's office to have chemo her BP was too low to have it. It continued to drop and her Oncologists' team rushed her to Rutherford Hospital via ambulance. I went directly to the hospital. When I stepped off the elevator Aunt Gail was standing there waiting on me. She was crying. She was one of my rocks and if she was upset then I knew something bad had happened. For a split second I thought Mama had passed but fortunately she was still with us. Aunt Gail said Mama was in trouble and her BP had dropped to 65/32. It was not looking good. They hurried me into her room. Her bed was inverted and her feet were elevated. The nurse in charge rushed me and asked me if Mama was DNR! Dayum! I was Mama's POA (power of attorney) and had to act quickly. Mama was in and out of consciousness. I got down in her face and looked her in her green eyes and asked her, "Mama do you want to be resuscitated if it comes to that or do you want me to let you go?" I was an inch from her face and she looked me in my green eyes and shook her head no and said, "No DNR. I want to live." The same woman that tried to kill herself approximately 13 times in her life looked me in the eye and said she was full code. H707119 wanted to live. Sum bitch-let's do this!

12/9/2013 Mama's Oncologist

PAST MEDICAL HISTORY:

1.   *Bipolar disorder.*
2.   *Peripheral arterial disease.*
3.   *Probable peripheral neuropathy.*
4.   *Asthma.*

PAST SURGICAL HISTORY

1.   *Gastric bypass.*
2.   *Cholecystectomy.*
3.   *Hysterectomy.*
4.   *Tonsillectomy.*
5.   *Vegas nerve stimulator upper right chest.*
6.   *Biliary drain tube.*
7.   *Port-a-cath right upper chest.*

Mama's Oncologist's notes: Ms. Robbins is a 64 year old woman with unresectable pancreatic cancer. She had presented with jaundice and was found to have a pancreatic head mass. Workup showed a mass encasing the portal vein (2.5 X 2.4 cm.) and she was not felt to be an operative candidate. She had a questionable node as well. She underwent percutaneous (needle under the skin) biliary drain placement as she could not have an ERCP (endoscopic ultrasound) with placement due to previous bypass surgery. Gemcitabine chemotherapy was started but after the first dose she stopped. She developed nausea and an obstructed biliary stint for which she was admitted to Presbyterian Hospital where she received a bilary stint and had the stint replaced. She received a second dose of gemcitabine on Nov. 27, 2013 and initially did well, but then came back to the office with profound weakness. She had no proceeding nausea, vomiting, fever, chills, abdominal pain or diarrhea, but she was noted to be hypotensive. She had been hypotensive at Presbyterian as well and required several days of aggressive fluid replacement.

At the time of her discharge, the patient is eating breakfast. She is comfortable and not having pain.

DISPOSITION:

Patient will be discharged to home with medicines listed in the medicine reconciliation discharge form. I will see her back in the office in one week. We are going to resume chemotherapy next week. I will arrange for home health care with physical therapy at her request and have asked palliative care to continue following as an outpatient.

FINAL DISPOSITION:

1. *Hypotension secondary to medications and dehydration.*
2. *Torsade's de pointes secondary to electrolyte imbalance and possible medications.*
3. *Nausea secondary to pancreatic cancer.*
4. *Hypokalemia and hypomagnesaemia.*
5. *Candida UTI.*

BP 72/46.
Weight gain 192 lbs.
Gained 10 pounds in 10 days.
Dehydrated and bloated legs-edema.
Low protein.
Rutherford Hospital Room 278.

Dec. 4, 2013
I stopped by DSS to get her food stamps updated.
She gets $36.00 a month.

Rutherford Hospital ICU.
BP systolic in the 60's. She is not her normal self. She is more slurred in her speech, unable to find the words that she is trying to say.

21 medicines:

Magic mouthwash, Symbicort (asthma), Lovenox (prevent blood clots), Neurontin (nerve pain), Topamax (migraines), Wellbutrin (depression), Cymbalta (depression), Trazodone (depression), Meclizine (vertigo), Bentyl (irritable bowel syndrome), Compazine (nausea), Geodon (depression), Zanaflex (muscle relaxer), Celebrex (arthritis), OxyR 5 oxycodone), OxyContin, Phenergan (nausea), Protonix (acid reflux), Normal saline, Zyrtec, Albuterol inhaler (asthma).

Review of systems is very difficult to obtain this morning as she is not really able to communicate very well. She states she is having pain in her legs but 5 minutes later is denying any pain. Record indicates a 40 lb. weight loss that started while dieting in July of this year. She complains of feeling dizzy. She is complaining of shortness of breath and pain in her legs with the edema. She uses a bedside commode (thank you Debbie Buchanan and American Cancer Society) at home, not because she can't breathe to get there, but more because of the pain in her legs. She will go short distances. Her companion reports that she has a good appetite (emphatically not true) and she has asked me a couple of times if she is going to be able to eat or what can she eat when you can understand what she is saying. She is on a clear liquid diet right now. He states she has not eaten since 10:00 yesterday. BP is 60's over 30's and 40's. She weighs 205 due to the edema. Edema is 2-3+ pitting. She appears jaundice. She is very lethargic. She is oriented to person and it is very difficult to complete the exam due to her slurred speech. Her eyes are open and she does look around the room.

ASSESSMENT:

Palliative care encounter with complex decision making needs.

PLAN:

I briefly discussed code status with her to see if this has been addressed before or explained to her. She said no one has brought it up or discussed with her before so as of right now she is full code. Hopefully we will be able to discuss this with him further as she stabilizes and may be able to make her wishes known. Currently she is receiving a fluid bolus (rapid infusion of intravenous fluids) for her hypotension and trying to be stabilized or transferred to ICU. Also, medicines are being adjusted for hypotension, may be possibly related to sedation. She received a dose of Geodon last night. It had been stopped in Charlotte. She was no longer taking Geodon because she had a similar episode in Presbyterian Hospital as she is having today. A call was placed to the physician's office that was in charge of her care to clarify the current medications that she is supposed to be taking. They are to return that call to her oncologist. Will continue to follow her with palliative care. I will add vancomycin to her allergy list.

Her vagus nerve stimulator was blocked. Patient states that when her psychiatrist left the county in 2006 no one else knew how to adjust her vagus nerve stimulator (a vagus nerve stimulator is a pacemaker type implant in the upper chest area and is used to treat epilepsy and treatment resistant depression).

Dec. 5, 2013

Whew BP dictates life. Oncologist discussed full code, CPR could cause ribs to get crushed or worse.   I'm seeing the ugly face of the C word.

Side effects.

Meds.

Tremors.

Terror.

Her eyes sunken and her body swollen but she is alive and she wants to fight.

So by God we are as ready as one can be to slay a giant.

A giant so great that the odds are 99 to 1 against her.

Whatever.

We are in it 'til the last breath is taken.

Days, weeks, months.

I am exhausted.

Good and evil are always at war.

Good men must choose *-Nelson Mandela*.

Dec. 9, 2013

WTH?
Bp nosedived last Tuesday at pre chemo blood work.
Emergency!
Took her to hospital.
Plummeted again Wed. when I got there.
Immediately took me to her room.
Her bed was inverted. Asked me if DNR.
I had to ask her and she said NO not DNR!
BP 65/32 ICU until Fri.
Speech better.
Exhausted from sitting up and PT yesterday.
Nausea back.
Visitors-Aunt Joy, Uncle Bill and Patsy Day.

Told me in her exhausted voice…..I love you so so so very much.
Need to speak to her oncologist about nausea, rehab, and hose for swollen legs.
Today I am struggling and cannot focus.
Anxiety high.
Call grief counselor to see me today?

Cold claws of winter squeezing at my heart. Her life clock is ticking and leaking like antifreeze.
Anything I can do for you?
Just love me.
I will love you until forever and beyond without condition.
Will you love me forever?
Yes.
Her sausage toes have gone down some.
Cannot go to rehab and cannot do chemo. Scratch that.
Oncologist wants chemo to be her priority-so here we go.

Her rules….for now.
Build a ramp they said….and so we will.
CT scan to check abdomen to see what's causing nausea.

Dec. 10, 2013

It was you and me and daddy made 3.
Your ages combined was 36 and some change.
One slipped away then there was one on the way.
Then our lives were filled with Joye.
Time marched on then Daddy was gone.
We had each other and held on tight.
A child raising children-we were a sight.
Most of the time we turned to Maw.
She was always there heeding the call.

You did what you could and you gave us your all.
From grade mom to washing my classmate's hair in the sink cause it needed it.
You gave her my clothes.
An example of compassion that I did not understand at five years old.
Oh but I do now mama.
From baton to cheerleading to pitching that ball.
You lead us through and were coach for us all.
We never knew the colors of skin.
We don't know it now and we didn't know it then.
You came to our games and held parties with our friends.
You took us skating and on wheels we could fly.
Daredevil girls-there was nothing we would not try.
Especially that least one-now that one's a mess.
Don't even try to put her in a dress.
No shirt and no shoes #2 knows best.
Times got lean and you taught me to be humble.
When your kids needed something you moved hell and high water.

December 10, 2013

ICU for heart rate.
Too low.
I am off to see mama.

Dec. 11, 2013

We made a promise we swore we'd always remember.
No retreat baby no surrender.
I am a weary traveler.
A pilgrim on my way to destinations unknown.
Funny how life takes over and you stop at a store just to poop cause ya gotta go cause your belly hurts from life taking over.

Dec. 18, 2013

The salt betrays my eyes again.
She will not eat.
Imagine.
A Honeycutt that will not eat. Blasphemy.

Dec. 19, 2013

Breath is labored.
Sat up today and walked a little. Ate cornbread and buttermilk.
Palliative care came to assess her.
Getting a hospital bed and PT at home.
Talked on the phone with her and I asked her the best thing that happened to her today and she thought for a second and said she met two new people today.

Dec. 21, 2013

Mawmaw always said to call your mama.
She misses you and she seems so sad.
I do maw.
I do.

Jan. 1, 2014

Back on track for chemo.
Weighed 172 pounds almost two weeks ago.
Wonder what her weight was yesterday.

It was 162 pounds.
"When tomorrow starts without me, save a place for me."

Jan. 2, 2014

Nurse said keep on doing same things.
PT today and biliary tube change in Charlotte tomorrow.

Jan. 8, 2014

Mama wants a big font bible.
Doing good.
Sounds stronger each day.
Working on fuel assistance with Rutherford County DSS. They came right away the same day when I told them she was a cancer patient. Thank you!

Jan. 11, 2014

Flee ghosts for now I love me.

Jan. 14, 2014

My love will never die.
My love will never cease.
My love will never die.

Jan. 17, 2014

153 lbs. OMG.
Some things never change.
They disguise themselves as horses or zebras but they never change.

Chapter 36- Verbatim

This is the verbatim text Mama sent me:

Texted me on 1/17/14 at 4:04 PM

Want it done
tired pleeaas hhelp
Used to ccould taakee it
Hhelpppp

I called Mama and I could tell she needed to go to the fifth floor Psychiatric Unit. I got her boyfriend on the phone and told him to take her immediately to the emergency room. I called Denita Reid Vickers who happens to be one of my favorite humans, our cousin, and a nurse at the local hospital. She lives on the way to the hospital from our homeplace on the hill. I asked her to secretly pull out behind them and follow them to the hospital. That was to ensure she made it to the hospital safely. When they got to the hospital and he went to park the car, they took Mama straight back into the ER treating area. Patient H707119 was now safe.

Section 4: Locked Out

Chapter 37- Even Without Her Glasses She is Starting to See

On Jan. 17, 2014 her boyfriend was locked out of her life forever. Just like that she was free. She made it clear to me that she didn't ever want to see him again. I ensured her that was the last time she would ever see him.

The ER Doctor states:

The patient is a 64 year old who was admitted voluntarily through our emergency room where she presented as anxious and increasingly depressed. The patient notes her depression has been getting much worse over the past 2-3 weeks and she has been having wishes to be dead (She knew the code words to use and she wanted out of her situation and relationship). She has been diagnosed with pancreatic cancer since being here the last time in July of 2013. She was hospitalized here in December for hypotension. During that hospitalization we lowered her Cymbalta and her Geodon was discontinued.

The patient notes that she is sad and feels hopeless and helpless. She is having problems with sleep with initial insomnia and awakens in the night and has difficulty returning to sleep. She is extremely fatigued during the day. She has been feeling more self-reproachful and often feels worthless. She has intensive depressive ideas of reference that often reach paranoid proportions and she has become severely anhedonic (without pleasure or depressed). She denies having any active suicidal intent or plan.

The patient is also irritable and short-tempered and has a lot of mood swings. She notes stress in life being her relationship with her boyfriend who has been abusive in the past. The patient notes high levels of anxiety and excessive worries. She denies having any panic attacks, obsessions, compulsions,

or psychotic symptoms. The patient denies any use of tobacco, alcohol, drugs, or excessive caffeine. Past medical history is pancreatic cancer, arthritis, and asthma. Family history is notable for cancer, diabetes, and cardiac issues.

On mental status exam, the patient appears her stated age and is moderately cooperative. She is extremely fatigued and has difficulty holding her eyes open. She is lying in the hospital bed. Psychomotor (body and brain coordination) activity levels are extremely slowed, and there is a significant increase in latency of response. The patient's mood is severely depressed and dysphonic (difficulty speaking). Affect is flattened. There is no evidence of any gross cognitive abnormalities as the patient is fully oriented and displays adequate memory. Given her fatigue and sleepiness it is difficult to fully test this. Her concentration and attention are impaired. There is no evidence of any psychotic process or disordered thinking. The patient reaches goal ideas with minimal difficulty. She denies homicidal ideations. Her judgment and insight are limited.

ADMITTING DIAGNOSIS

AXIS I: Major depression, recurrent, and severe, with passive suicidal ideations. Anxiety disorder, not otherwise specified.

AXIS II: Personality disorder, not otherwise specified.

AXIS III: Pancreatic cancer, asthma, arthritis.

AXIX IV: Moderate to severe psychosocial stressors.

AXIS V: GAF upon admission 20 (global assessment of psychological, social, and occupational) functioning on a scale of 0-100 with 100 being the highest.

We will continue to monitor the patient on every 15 minute checks initially. Lab work and her past chart have been reviewed. We have not checked a magnesium which she had trouble with at last admission. At her last admission she also had tortes de pointes due (irregular heartbeat) due to electrolyte abnormalities. We will repeat EKG. We will also check a B12 which has been 101 in the past as well as a ferritin and iron series as she has demonstrated iron deficiency in the past as well.

The patient is having poor p.o. (oral) intake and we will give her Ensure Plus between meals. After reviewing the EKG, we will consider potentially increasing her Cymbalta and consider augmentation strategies (strategies to change a behavior). We might consider increasing Wellbutrin. I consulted with the oncologist who is covering for her oncologist over the weekend. We discussed the anemia and the platelets which are consistent with chemotherapy. I will consult with her oncologist on Monday regarding any additional medical treatment that is indicated. We will continue to monitor the patient's vital signs, which currently do not demonstrate any hypotension, for potential development of such. I encouraged the patient to drink and eat to maintain adequate fluid intake.

DISCHARGE SUMMARY

Her oncologist was consulted and he ordered additional lab work. This revealed severe anemia with a hemoglobin of 7.8. The patient continues to be weak, sad, and depressed. Her blood pressure started trending downward and given her severe depression and wishes to be dead, her Cymbalta was switched to Prestiq. She tolerated the Pristiq well without adverse side effects. Her mood gradually began to improve over the next couple of days. She stopped having wishes to be dead and her times of feeling hopeless and helpless diminished. She had good visits with her daughter and her blood pressure improved due to the switch to Prestiq. Her weight on December 13, 2013 was 216 lbs. due to edema. On January 17, 2014 she weighed 153 lbs. In little over a month she lost 63 pounds.

DISCHARGE DIAGNOSIS

AXIS I: Major depression recurrent, severe, and improved, anxiety disorder not otherwise specified.

AXIS II: Personality disorder not otherwise specified.

AXIS III: Pancreatic cancer, anemia, asthma, arthritis.

AXIS IV: Moderate to severe stressors.

AXIS V: GAF upon discharge 65.

DISCHARGE MEDICATIONS-1/22/14:

Nentolin inhaler (asthma), Symbicort (asthma), Wellbutrin (depression), Pristiq (depression), Digoxin (heart failure), Marinol (nausea), Flonase, Levaquin (antibiotic), Imodium, Ativan (anxiety), Mag-Ox (indigestion), Reglan (nausea), Metoprolol (angina), Ensure Plus, Omeprazole (acid reflux), Klor-Con (low potassium), Prochlorperazine (nausea), Topomax (migraines), Trazadone (depression). She was on 19 medications.

Chapter 38- I will Repay You for the Years the Locusts Have Eaten

Jan. 19, 2014

5th floor what's she gonna do? What is Mama gonna choose? She is in charge.

She needed time and space to get herself together or not. She was insistent that she see her psychiatrist and adamant that she didn't want to go back to the homeplace on the hill. I went to see her on Sunday evening. There were several beds in the room but she was by herself. Mama looked tiny in the big room with multiple vacant beds lined up like an evacuated Army barracks. She looked pretty good considering what she was going through. I was thankful to see her and terrified for her. Visiting hours were limited so I called her several times a day. The psychiatric unit staff was great about getting the phone to her. They would literally take her a phone so she could talk to her family.

Tragically, one of the nurses stepped on her glasses and broke them. That must have been awful. No one got them fixed and she could barely see anything without them. So there she was with terminal and rapid cancer, in the psychiatric unit, and now she cannot see with her eyes. I tried to buy her some over the counter glasses but she had to have special ones with a prism in them. I tried to order her new ones but they said she had to come in to be fitted. Really? We pieced them together and they held up.

Her oncologists, psychiatrist, and mama decided no more chemo. Mama had more decisions to make. She would be getting out of the psychiatric unit soon and she needed to decide where she was going. When she was in ICU in Rutherford Hospital, a lady named Ronda Patton came to visit her. Ronda was with Hospice of Rutherford County. Aunt Joy and Uncle Bill (Mawmaw's brother) were also there visiting. Ronda reminded Mama that she had stage 4 cancer. No one had really came out and said that before. Ronda asked Mama if she would be interested in palliative or hospice care. A DNR (do not resuscitate) is usually a part of the hospice process. Mama had a devastated and sad reaction to that information. Aunt Joy told me that Mama's expression was the saddest thing she had ever seen. Mama told Ronda that she was not interested. In fact at that point we still had some hope for Mama's recovery. We were angry with Ronda. Hospice equaled death in our minds. That was a place where people go to die. Boy, were we ignorant!

Jan. 20, 2014

7469 Mama's psych. unit code. Dreamed
she was plump.
Hair was longer and permed.
Her teeth were white and she was smiling.
Grief counseling for me today.
Need some insight.

Jan. 21, 2014

One time too many.
She left me.

Jan. 22, 2014

Left you last night with no tears and hope in my heart.
You wanted to go to rehab and we made a plan.
You signed the papers.
Today your hemoglobin is 7 and you want to fold your cards.
Hold on Mama the blood is coming. The transfusion is on its way from Charlotte to
you. Tomorrow Hospice or Nursing Care-you can decide.

Jan. 24, 2014

828-247-8778
Hospice House.
Rough one.
I can't stop crying.
Hdn west.
Mama.
I cannot rescue her this time.
Lisa Rosier thank you.

Chapter 39- She is Yours Ronda

Upon dismissal from the hospital, consultation was obtained with Ronda Patton of the palliative care services. The patient stated that she wished to go to rehabilitation at hospice, and given her need for a transfusion, she was discharged from our unit to have an outpatient blood transfusion. The patient was subsequently discharged in fair condition from a psychiatric standpoint with a regular diet and activity ad lib.

She asked the doctor to contact me to inform me of her decision. She also asked them to put her now ex-boyfriend on a do not visit list to which they obliged. She stated she will be making all of her own decisions moving forward. She understands the outcome of stopping treatments. She wants to be comfortable. She wants to be DNR.

After consulting with her doctors and me, Mama decided she would go to hospice for what we thought was palliative and or rehabilitation. On January 23, 2014 on a Friday morning, Mama was transported via ambulance to Hospice House of Rutherford County. Aunt Joy beat her there to ensure Mama knew she was loved, important, and not alone. However, when Mama arrived she was almost catatonic and was barely speaking. She didn't engage in conversation and would only answer the nurse's questions. Her affect was flat. She was terrified, highly depressed, and wouldn't make eye contact. She was calm, withdrawn, and quiet. Her pain was an 8 on a scale of 10 being the worst. On intake she was 5' 7" and 153 lbs. Prior to this sickness Mama was 5'9" and over 220 lbs. Later in Mama's journey the Hospice doctor told me he didn't think Mama would live through that first weekend.

Mama was moved into the Lilac suite. All the suites were named after flowers or trees. Her room was like an upscale hotel suite. She was at the end of the hall so she had a little extra privacy. Each suite had a full bath in it. There was a three quarter wall that divided the large room. It had a pull out sofa bed and a quaint little kitchenette in it. Family and friends were encouraged to sleep over and stay as long as they wanted.

Mama met Chaplain Cecelia the second day of her stay. The spiritual concerns Mama voiced to Cecelia were uncertainty and anxiety. Dr. M. was one of Mama's doctors at Hospice House. Five days after intake Dr. M. noticed Mama was sitting up in bed, alert, fairly responsive, and in fairly good spirits. She assured Mama that she would be present and support her. Aunt Joy and Aunt Gail were also there to support Mama and reassure her that they were going to be there for her and they were. Mama had also started to greet each employee by name when they came into her room. She started drinking liquids a little as well as smiling slightly.

Right away Mama's care was off the charts. The CNA's and nurses took magnificent care of her. They stopped often to check on her or to see if they could get her anything. Every employee there was trained to say "Let us know if you need anything" as they left the room. The food was exquisite and the chef could do some cooking. Mama could eat or not eat, drink or not drink. She had her very own remote control and she could watch anything she wanted on TV. Mama was still losing weight and physically getting weaker but her spirits were rising! She was invited to go for walks or get in the jacuzzi tub or go sit by the big fireplace in the living room. She was 100% in control of her life, her situation, and her remote control!

Upon arrival at Hospice House she was on 23 medications. She had tried to commit suicide about 13 times. She was in ICU once and almost succeeded. She had been in the Psychiatric Unit at Kings Mountain NC, Park Ridge NC, Gastonia NC, Spartanburg SC, Baptist in Richland County, SC, Bull Street SC, Killingsworth Halfway House SC, Charter Hospital of Greenville, SC, and Rutherford Hospital, NC, more times than I could count. She had been misdiagnosed multiple times. She had tried a vagus nerve implant, hypnosis, electric shock therapy, psychiatric counseling, vocational rehabilitation, outpatient rehabilitation and more medications than one can fathom. After all of that it took just 7 days of kindness and love and treating her like a medical patient instead of a mental patient for her affect to go from flat to normal. H707119 ceased to exist any longer. Mama was becoming the person she was born to be. We were seeing flashes of getting our Mama back. She was alive and just maybe there was hope blooming in our family garden again. Was she on the verge of becoming a beacon?

Not too long after Mama went to Hospice House Aunt Joy's birthday rolled around. I bought Mama several bags of flower seeds and a card for her to give. I helped her sign the card and assisted her in putting the items in the bag. She was grateful to be able to give Aunt Joy a birthday gift. It took her a while to get the paper in the gift bag and then place the card and seeds in the bag. She was quite pleased with herself and happy. That was one of many things she taught me during her stay at Hospice House. Little things like a .99 cent bag of flower seeds can be better than big things sometimes. After Mama gave Aunt Joy her gift, I looked over at them and they were holding hands. Two grown women, aunt and niece looked like two precious little girls holding on for dear life. Looking back, maybe they were.

About a week after Mama went to Hospice House, the same doctor that on admission thought Mama might not make it through the weekend said "Her psychiatric issues have dramatically improved and she has developed a comfort level here that has put her at peace." We were all witnessing a transformation literally in front of our eyes. Chaplain Cecelia also stated "She was in good spirits, sharing about family who have been providing support and spoiling her." "I will repay you for the years the locusts have eaten" was the Bible verse Chaplain Cecilia told me that personified Mama's transformation from being broken and transformed into a beacon.

Jan. 26, 2014

Spent Friday night with mama.
We had a good time.
Dr. H. said maybe a month or less.
Not eating today.
Her voice sounded weak.
She said she rested good.

Jan. 27, 2014

Her body is not cooperating.
Cannot control her functions and cannot walk.
SSI and social worker.
Holly Springs?

Chapter 40- Zebras

On January 27, 2014, Mama told me he had sex with her in December. Listening to her tell me that was painful. I watched her tell me as tears rolled down her face. There was something different about Mama though. She was calmer, relaxed, forgiven, and forgiving. It was as if she released the pain. However, I caught it and that image was burned in my head and infuriated me beyond any words I could find. She also told me she felt bad for him as a human being. After all she had allowed him to put her through she was telling me she felt sorry for him. She was quiet and soft spoken as she told me. She repeated she didn't want to see him. As God was my witness I promised her that would never happen as long as that was what she wanted. He never saw her again. I made sure of that.

He did show up one night after midnight wanting to see her. I was sitting up asleep and one of Mama's precious nurses, Courtney called me to come down to the nurse's desk. He had gotten in. I refused to let him see her and told him that she still didn't want to see him. I also told him that if he ever cared for her or our family at all that he would leave and never contact us again. I never told her he came by. There was no way I was going to allow her to be insecure or afraid ever again. I would have done anything necessary to ensure that happened. When I said anything that is exactly what I meant. She had security and peace and I would not allow anyone or anything to disrupt her journey home. I had the support of HH in that endeavor. He was on a do not visit list. Mama was in complete control and guiding the way. She had a team of people surrounding her that were determined to protect her and keep her feeling secure. I had forgiven him once for helping to destroy my family when I was a child. Fool me twice is shame on me. Neither heaven nor hell would stop me from stopping him from contacting her in any fashion.

There was also another old friend of hers that she didn't want to see. Mama had gently told me she didn't want to be bossed around ever again. She felt that particular friend was too overbearing and not good energy to be around. Mama was softly demanding to be released from drama. Eventually that old friend came around and she and Mama reconciled on Mama's terms. Mama was honest with her about why she didn't want to see her. Mama ran from confrontation her entire life. She never stood up for herself. In fact there was a time that she would do anything to keep from confronting someone she cared about even if they were treating her like crap. It was just not possible for her to do even though that was not a rational reaction. It was however her reality. Mama was evolving.

I contacted Aunt Patsy and another old friend of Mama's, Peggy Mask. Mama hadn't seen them in a month of Sundays (a significant amount of time) and was thrilled to catch up with them. They visited her on a regular basis. It was nostalgic and magical to see the three of them catching up and hanging out. They acted like three teenagers catching up on life. It was beautiful to watch and be a part of. There was something spiritual and soul stirring about it.

Jan. 27, 2014

Eric sing.
Deb do service about peace.
Peace that passes all understanding.

Her visitors were plentiful. One day one of her amazing CNA's, Christy and I talked her into getting in the Jacuzzi tub. She reluctantly agreed. I was so glad. She had a prized visitor coming and I wanted her to look nice. We wheeled her down the hall and they lowered her into the Jacuzzi tub. She loved it! It felt good on her skin and bones. When she was ready to get out, another special CNA Lisa, had brought her a choice of a couple of different things to wear. She chose a pink Shadowline gown. She looked like an angel. A sick and scrawny angel. Her eyes were starting to get sunken and her broken but patched up glasses were getting too large for her face. Regardless, she looked radiant and beautiful.

Mama had some treasured visitors that day. An old friend from our community, Starlyn Sims Whisnant (she grew up in the curve where Mama totaled her red Chevy Malibu), Reverend's Jackie and Debbie Potter, and me and Mama sat by the fireplace in the big and beautiful living room. We prayed and told stories and held hands. It was a gathering of love and good will. That is where Mama's relationship with Debbie and Jackie took off like a rocket ship. Debbie is Mama's niece by marriage. Debbie's Mama and my Daddy are brother and sister.

That would be the first and last time Mama ever left her room. I was grateful for the beauty of seeing her smile. It left her dog tired but it was worth every precious second. Little did she know her baby girl was coming to see her that evening. That might have been one of the best days if not the best day of Mama's life.

Mama always made friends fast and easy. It came natural to her. Sometimes the CNA's and nurses would visit her on their day off or at the end of their shift. One day it appeared Mama was retaining fluid more so than usual. One of the CNA's said "Barbara it looks like your private parts are a little puffy and swollen today." Mama said "I have always had a perky pussy". She had not lost her crazy sense of humor. Her girls fell out laughing.

Jan. 30, 2014

Angels among us.
I cry for her exit.
I cry for her anxiety.
I cry for the angels.

Feb. 1, 2014

Heading west to see mamacuz.
Michaels for handouts-seashells and stones.
Paper and twine.
Template to cut out doves or seashells.
My breaths are deep cause hers are labored and my anxiety is high.
Second pain meds since I got here.
Gatorade, buttermilk, lifesavers, People magazine.
Hard to plan someone's funeral when they are alive and laying right beside you.
She told me she had to get her driver's license renewed in May.
Chest hurts cause she will be in heaven by then but I ain't saying that out loud.

Feb. 6, 2014

Crossword puzzle.
People magazine and buttermilk.
Bags and paper.
Large font women's Bible.
Aussie shampoo and conditioner.
Nurses Peggy, Dee, Courtney.
Buttermilk queen.
Drank 2 glasses in the night.
Guts hurt cause her guts hurt.
No depression in heaven.
Take my hand precious lord.
Amazing Grace/My Chains Are Gone.
Life's evening sun.
Carolina Girls.

Feb. 6, 2014

Heading west.

DNR.
Gets to stay at Hospice House!

YES!

After Mama was at Hospice House of Rutherford County for a few weeks her symptoms were somewhat managed. At that point we were hoping for her to go into resident status. That meant she would no longer be a short-term patient but would become a resident and remain at Hospice House for the rest of her days. There was an impending obstacle. There were no beds available. Mama had flourished beyond recognition from when she entered the Hospice doors. Everyone could see it. Her doctor was highly impressed and quite frankly surprised. Her PA (Ronda Patton) could see it and didn't want her to have to leave. Her social worker Danielle was also determined to help me get Mama's fate sealed.

I never told Mama but at one point I had to look into other potential care facilities. I checked with several nursing facilities in the county and they were not quick to respond.

I met with Mama's social worker Danielle again and she set up an appointment with another facility to see if Mama was a good fit. They came and interviewed her. After a day or so I called Danielle to see what was going on. Mama had the "MI" (Mental Illness) by her name and no one would take her and by law they didn't have to. She was legally being discriminated against. The law was exclusionary and unjust. The stigma was trying to work its way back into her life. No one at Hospice even knew about her mental illness because no one could tell! None of us were ashamed of it but it had suddenly become a topic of conversation that was just not a part of our daily lives anymore.

While out looking for a possible placement for Mama, I checked out a care facility in our community. One of the ladies that worked there asked me if I had heard that Mama's belongings were being sold out of her house. I had not heard anything about that and I did not check into it. Oddly her "belongings" were no longer material possessions instead her "belongings" were me and Joye. I got it. I understood what was taking place within Mama and my priorities were Mama's priorities.

Dr. H, Ronda Patton, Danielle, myself, and a host of other people rallied to figure out how we could keep Mama at Hospice which was quickly becoming her new home. On February 6, 2014 I received a call from Dr. H. As fate would have it a bed had become available and I literally fell to my knees in thanks. It was solidified. Mama was a resident and would fly away from Hospice when she was called home. The joy and gratitude was almost too much. She deserved this and so it was to be. How blessed and fortunate we were that none of the other nursing care facilities wanted her. Hospice wanted her and that was the most wonderful thing that could have happened. That was one of the happiest days of my life. We were walking in high cotton. Just Barbara was blooming.

Feb. 10, 2014

She said she craved green apples when I was in her belly.

Feb. 13, 2014

Talked to Mama twice.
Ready to see her and spend some precious time.
She said Rob I love you.

Feb. 14, 2014

Alternate Routes.
We are how we treat each other.

Feb. 19, 2014

17 Visitors today.

Feb. 21, 2014

At DSS applying for special assistance for Mama (Medicaid stuff).
Old building.

Feb. 22, 2014

Stayed Wed, Thurs, Fri.
Little incoherent.
Dr. H says let her be as long as she is not frightened.
Be right back Mama.
20 Visitors.

Feb. 23, 2014

Tracy Chapman
At this point in my life.

Feb. 24, 2014

Heading west.
She asked me to come.
Says she needs me.
I am taking the outdoors to her-leaves, a feather, and acorns.
She smiled huge when I brought her crisp bacon.
Free like a bird is what she told me.
Good lord willin' and the creek don't rise
I'll be hittin' Rutherford County by supper time.

Feb. 25, 2014

Buttermilk. Sprite. G2. Diet Mountain Dew.

Feb. 28, 2014

SSI $115.00 and disability $615.00

March 1, 2014

"Faith is a bird that feels dawn breaking and sings while it is still in the dark." Rabindranath Tagore
Great visit. To see her happy and smile, and whole, and peaceful, and forgiven….
Aunt Joy taking her hand just to hold on to it.
Debbie and Jackie praying and Jackie telling Mama she is beautiful. Redeemed!
Hospice House saved her life!

March 6, 2014

Edema is causing significant swelling in her legs. Stop the Pepsi's?
Keep those Pepsi's coming, let her indulge.
Thank you Mama's Courtney for keeping me in check.
Let her have whatever she wants.
Mama had a good night.

Slept well.
Heart hurts.
I am Taylor tough.
Endure and smile......breath.

March 8, 2014

Be not inhospitable to strangers lest they be angels. *- W.B. Weats*

March 9, 2014

Left you sleepy.
Time lept forward and we lost a precious hour that no money could buy.
I asked you to enjoy every minute of every day.
You held my head and you ate pizza.
The buttermilk queen.
The baconator.
I called to see if you had eaten.
No answer.
Hoping you are sleeping.
Taking care of things for you and hoping I can salvage my own self and not end up for sale
at Goodwill.
Beautiful day and yesterday I opened your door and you closed your eyes and felt fresh air, heard
birds, and church bells. You closed your eyes and drank it in like a horse at a trough after a long
steamy ride through the desert.
6 Visitors.
I know you miss me.
Told ya I gotta make kibble money.

March 14, 2014

.41 cents per word he said. That's what the guy at the newspaper told me about obituaries.

Her pain was minimal but her discomfort would come and go. She developed a bedsore that caused her irritation but they treated it and her CNA's aka her girls, kept her turned often. Nausea was the demon she could not lick. It would rear its ugly head regularly. She was treated with every anti-nausea medication you could think of. It would curb it for a while but sometimes it got pretty bad. Once it got the best of her. Mama's Courtney called me one morning real early and told me that Mama had a rough night. She said she started to call me to come there but they worked it out. Mama was so nauseous that she got overwhelmed and asked her Courtney straight out if she was dying. Courtney held her and rocked her like a baby and told her no she wasn't dying. Courtney was 23 years old and held my Mama. She soothed her and reassured her that it wasn't time to go yet. Sweet Courtney. Mama's Courtney. No Mama it wasn't your time yet. Thank you God for sending Mama angels disguised in nurses clothes.

We tried everything under the sun to help Mama eat. Anything she wanted was hers to be had. She asked for cornbread and milk every day for weeks. Different visitors would bring her homemade cornbread. Aunt Joy cooked for her often and made sure Mama never ran out of cornbread. Aunt Gail would surprise her with her homemade cornbread too. Yeah! She finally found some food she could tolerate. She became known as the cornbread queen. Her next food fetish was crisp bacon from Bojangle's. She then affectionately became known as the baconator. She could eat ten pieces at a time. She then jumped around a bit when it came to food. She called me one day and asked me to stop at Arby's and get her a Reuben and a Dr. Pepper. Sometimes it was just oddly humorous. Her cravings were delightful to hear about because her nausea nemesis often deprived her of food. Our people (Honeycutt's) are food loving people. Honeycutt women have a proven reputation of being phenomenal southern cooks. Mama not wanting food was the exact opposite of who we were. She struggled to get protein in her dwindling body. I often teased her about taking her "Honeycutt" card away from her. Everyone knows Honeycutt women can do some cooking and we all love to eat!

One afternoon Aunt Gail, Aunt Joy, Denita, her daughter Alex, and myself were hanging out with Mama. I started singing a song to Mama called Boney Maroney because for the first time in her life she was skinny. Not unfat. Not slim. Skinny. Anyway, Alex didn't believe it was a real song. I looked it up on YouTube and started playing it. Aunt Gail jumped up and she and I started dancing for Mama. We were cutting up and acting a fool. We sang along to that crazy song while we were cutting a rug. If Mama would have been able, she would have danced with us. Mama always loved to dance and let me tell ya the gal had rhythm.

The big day came when the Tarheels would play the Bluedevils. Mama and I were devout Tarheel fans. A few years back Mama had bought some fleece cloth with Tarheel print on it. She made a blanket out of it for my Christmas gift. I was snuggled up in it that night. I helped her put on her Tarheel shirt and hat and then I put mine on. We were excited about the game. We cheered and fussed at the TV. The score didn't really matter much to us that night. What we were really doing was making a memory together and cheering on our Tarheels.

A dear family friend (and one of my second mom's), Mama Liz Freeman had Mama a Tarheel wreath made for the door of her room. We hung it up and it looked great. Sometimes Mama Liz would come by just to sit with Mama and me. She would bring homemade cakes to entice Mama and spoil me. Her chocolate cake would make you want to slap your granny.

Mama had so many visitors that a few times we had to rotate them out of her room. Kinfolk and old friends showed up in droves to see Mama. She was overwhelmed and she told the Aunts she had no idea that many people loved her. Once she had twenty in one day. Aunt Joy and Aunt Gail were fixtures in Mama's room. At times it seemed as though Aunt Joy had moved in with Mama. She had relatives that she hadn't seen in years come by and love on her. Daddy's nieces came to visit. Old friends and now grown up children that Mama coached came to see her. Skating rink friends from our youth and people in the community appeared in numbers. Gina Tate came to hang out with Mama and talk about the old days (she didn't bring her cool light brown skates though). My childhood friend, Lori Toney, brought her dog Coop for Mama to love on. Mama Liz's baby girl and my old special friend Missy Limerick came by to remind Mama how much she was loved. Our sweet Denise Greene (Neicy) came by to bring the ocean to Mama. Mama and Mawmaw always said "ain't nobody like Neicy". She gave Mama a CD with ocean sounds, CD player with headset, an ornate miniscule beach chair with real sand underneath it, and an umbrella on it.

Everyone that knew Mama knew she had an obsession and love for "the beach". She and I had talked about me taking her to the beach in February. I'm not sure why she picked that month. I encouraged her even though I knew she would not be able to travel.

Hospice volunteers came by regularly to visit. One of the volunteers that Mama got close to was a guy that played guitar. He would come and play and sing for her. Mama looked forward to his visits. They had a bond that was evident and it was obviously spiritual. He would sing to her and she would look him right in the eyes while listening to him intently. She once told me, "Rob, I looked him in the eyes and held his stare. I never do that." He knew her situation and he was more than willing to visit Mama. In fact, he would end up playing again for her one last time at her celebration of life. Mama was suddenly surrounded with good men with no agenda. She was relishing it. She was also becoming the person she was born to be. Mama was completely in control of her remote for the TV. Whatever she flipped it to I would quietly sit and watch it with her. I had never watched so much reality TV in my life! We watched Myrtle Manor (because it was about a Myrtle Beach trailer park), Pitbull Parolee, and Here Comes Honey Boo Boo. Lord have mercy on me. I was fighting the good fight so I would snuggle down in my chair beside her under my Tarheel blanket and watch those crazy shows with her. Truthfully, I liked Pitbull Parolee. Shhhhhhh.

Chapter 41- Finding Elisha

Mama thrived on the attention and being taken care of. She got especially close with several of the HH workers. One of her girls, Lisa confided in her about her own losses. Mama's Nurse Ashley brought her baby to visit on her day off work. Another one of her sweethearts, Erica, brought her three little kids to visit Mama after work one day.

Nurse Peggy and Mama also had a special relationship. Peggy was a beautiful woman with exceptionally pretty features. She always wore all white uniforms that made her look angelic. Mama had been noticing a charm on Peggy's bracelet and eventually she asked her about it. Peggy told her it was for her little grandbaby boy Elisha who had gone on to heaven. Several weeks later as Mama got sicker Peggy was her nurse for the night and I happened to be there. Mama asked Peggy about Elisha again. Peggy told us she would be right back. She left Mama's room and returned a few minutes later with her iPad. She had some pictures of Elisha and she shared them with Mama and me. There was one photo that Mama kept staring at. She slowly started tracing his features with her finger. Her movements were meticulous and deliberate. Her touch moved gracefully around his little mouth and eyes. I eventually asked her what she was doing. She told Peggy and me she was trying to make sure she could remember his face so she could find him for her when she got to heaven. She and Peggy remained very close. Mama was finding peace and she wanted to do something for her sweet Peggy.

Mama wanted to give something back to everyone that had been so good to her. She asked me what could she do to give back. So I went to the craft section at Walmart (my least favorite place on the planet) and bought a bag of charms. I got seashells, crosses, angel wings, sand dollars, and starfish. Mama had an obsession with Myrtle Beach and that theme seemed to fit. I bought her a small silver lace mesh pouch to put her charms in. Anyone that came through her door for the first time would receive a charm from her. She would pick it out herself and give them what she wanted them to have. Sometimes I would have to remind her and she would say "Oh yeah". I would hand her the bag and she would gently and diligently open the bag and pick out a charm for her guest. That was a slow process and sometimes a physical challenge for her but she wanted to give something to her visitors. It was important to her. She had received so much and she needed to give back and show her gratitude.

I wanted to give back to Hospice House for Mama. I noticed that volunteers from different organizations would donate "tray treats" for the meal trays. I had hundreds of nature photos that I had taken over the years. I brought some in for Mama to see and I put some on her wall along with the cards and letters she had received. It was the wall we decorated for each holiday as well. It was covered with love. She and I went through some of the pictures together and we decided to give a bunch of them to the chef to put on the meal trays as a treat. Each person would get a picture of a rose, sunset, bright leaf, or any of the other many nature photos we donated. We needed to share the copious amount of love and gratitude we were experiencing.

On March 23, 2014 our sweet little cousin Katie Reid (Aunt Gail's granddaughter) had her wedding shower. Mama wanted to give Katie something special to remember her by. She said to me, "Rob, what if we loan Katie mama's wedding band and she could incorporate it into her bouquet and me and mama could walk her down the aisle?" Wow! Now that was a great idea. Katie loved Mawmaw Betty and Mama. Mama had worn Mawmaw's wedding band since Mawmaw passed.

She had lost so much weight during her sickness that her rings didn't fit any longer. She took them off and asked me to put them up for a special occasion. Katie's wedding shower was that special occasion. When Katie opened her gift she was overwhelmed. She was grateful and happy that Mama thought of her and wanted to be at her wedding with her even if it was through a spiritual gesture. Katie also wrote Mama's name on a chalkboard in the foyer of the church on her wedding day. She wanted Mama to be there and Katie felt Mama's presence.

Chapter 42- Please Take Care of My Girls

Mama got to where she would ask Aunt Joy repeatedly if she would look after her girls. She became obsessed with ensuring me and Joye were going to be taken care of. Aunt Joy would leave the room and she could hear Mama softly calling after her. She would go back and Mama would say "You are going to take care of my girl's aren't ya?" We were both in our forties and independent but Mama worried about us. At the end of her life all that mattered to her was me and Joye. Aunt Joy and Aunt Gail told her repeatedly that they would take care of us.

An interesting observation that myself and Aunt Joy noticed was Mama seemed to get better once I walked in the door. I don't know if I took her mind off of things or if by my being there soothed her somehow. She needed me but mostly she finally just wanted to make sure we were taken care of. The person who involuntarily sought to destroy me saved my soul and now because of her I will not fail. I cannot fail. Because of her I see that I am blessed with God's favor. What a gift she gave me!

She had no clothes at Hospice and never asked for any. She had no money and she didn't care. She had no car and she never asked about her house, she honestly didn't care about anything that was a material item. It simply became irrelevant. She did ask me about her 4 dogs and 3 cats once. I reassured her that I found great homes for all of her animals. She trusted me and never second guessed that I would handle everything correctly, respectfully, and responsibly. Nothing mattered to her except her two girls. The unconditional love was pouring out of her room. She became the person and the Mama she was born to be. I had learned to love her from arm's length over the years and hope was only a dream. But I had completely forgiven her several years ago. I knew I was now forever changed and I would live my life with a grateful heart because of Mama's journey. I was in the presence of a miracle straight from the hand of God. At times Mama exuded so much love it felt Holy. The undeniable peace and light radiated from her room, down the hall, out into the street, and all over our world.

I came in to visit Mama late one night. Aunt Patsy had left some pictures for me to look at. There was a picture of Mama and Daddy together before I was born. I was the upbeat, positive, and strong woman that always kept it together. When I saw that picture I was overpowered. I had never seen a picture of my parents together before. Plus the fact that Daddy had recently passed and I was looking at my terminal Mama it was too much. I started crying and I couldn't stop. I bawled my eyes out. I laid my head down on Mama's chest and she just let me cry. "You cradled me and held my hand and held my heart and when it was time you let me go."

Her telephone conversations with Joye were often and lengthy. Sometimes Mama's room was full of talkative visitors. She would get frustrated if it got too loud for her to hear her baby girl on the other end of the phone. So we worked out a signal that she was to use to let us know when it got too loud in the room. She would politely give us the thumbs up and we knew that meant to quiet or clear the room and that included me. She was adamant that she talk to and hear her youngest daughter as often as possible. As Mama got sicker she would hold on to the phone after she and her baby girl finished talking and disconnected. One time in particular she would not let go of the phone. She had it clutched like a vice grip. Her eyes were staring upward. I let her hold on to it as long as she wanted to that time because it seemed to be important to her to just hold on to baby girl. She pulled me close to her one night and grabbed my hand. She made me pinky swear that I would always look out for her baby girl. We locked pinkies and I swore to her that I would.

Once when she and I were talking on the phone, she told me that when we had her celebration of life and I was behind the pulpit talking about her that she would be there. I said I know you will and she said no really I will be there. I asked her if I could share some things with her and she said yes. I told her she wasn't having a church service and she said where then. I told her it would be held at Hospice Conference Center. She was overjoyed and overwhelmed. I told her she would not have a headstone and that I had gotten her a brick on the walkway leading into Hospice. I told her my childhood friend Eric Wilson was going to sing for her. That was as much as we discussed about that. It was too raw and too real. She was satisfied, overwhelmed and ecstatic about the plans. She let me know that Jackie and Debbie Potter were to be a major part of her celebration.

On March 22, 2014 Mama's ex called me and asked me why the electricity had been turned off in the house. How the hell would I know? He was supposedly staying there and taking care of the animals. He was staying there for free. I was angry! I didn't know the electricity was in danger of being cut off. He explained to me that they stayed a month behind and therefore the second month was past due and it had been disconnected. I later found a disconnect notice stating that a payment of $127.57 must be paid by March 13, 2014 or it would be disconnected. That was nine days ago and he was just then notifying me? It started to click in my head. He hadn't been staying there. I shouldn't have been surprised, yet I was. Mama's four dogs and three cats needed immediate attention.

Aunt Joy picked me up from Hospice House on the morning of March 22, 2014. She took me to the homeplace on the hill to help Mama's babies and pick up one of them and take her to the vet. Chloe was a tiny Chihuahua that Mama had rescued somewhere from somebody. My first cousin on Daddy's side, Diane Taylor wanted to adopt her. I had to do the right thing and take Chloe to the vet for a checkup and shots because she had never been to a vet. My dear friend Neicy met Aunt Joy and me at the homeplace on the hill. When all three of us walked in a sickening stench permeated the air. The odor was overpowering and it reeked of neglect and near death. The house had smelled awful for years but that was a new and higher level of foulness. It was a smell that caused gagging and breathing masks to be put on, disposable rubber gloves to be used, guts to hurt, and hearts to be broken. It was too much. There was a cat litter box on a table that had so much shit in it that it poured out of the box, onto the table, and onto the floor. There was very little, if any, food and water.

Those babies meant more to Mama than anything except Joye and me. She didn't or couldn't take them to the vet for their usual checkups and ailments. She did however ensure they were warm, dry, fed, and loved.

Mama's housekeeping was way passed bad but this scene was like something out of a revolting and sorrowful horror movie. There was no way I was going to let Mama find out about that fiasco. Chloe was so dehydrated that when we gave her water, her legs cramped up as if she was having a mini seizure. To say those babies were glad to see us was an understatement. The cats had been left alone and ignored for so long that they were somewhat feral inside the house. They would hide whenever I tried to get them to check on them. They would only come out for food and water. One of the cats was Mawmaw's, one was Mama's, and one belonged to her ex. Mawmaw's cat, Morris bolted out the door as soon as we opened it. I didn't blame him. I wanted to run away too! Fortunately he came back home and I was able to get him to his forever home. I was blessed enough to find a foster home for the other two. Oddly enough traps had to be set inside the house in order to capture them. They eventually came around and became lap kitties again.

Neicy took Greta and Scooter to her own vet in Charlotte, NC. Both dogs were rescues that Mawmaw and Mama had taken in years before. Greta was a purebred of some sort that a friend had given her and Scooter was Mawmaw's baby. She looked like Lady from Lady and The Tramp. Greta's checkup went well. She received her shots, etc. and was taken to her forever home. Scooter was about sixteen years old and in bad shape. She was matted, almost blind, arthritic to the point she could not walk well, and heartworm positive. Neicy had the daunting task of sending Scooter to her forever home in heaven. She was to be reunited with Mawmaw and now she would have to patiently sit at heaven's gate and wait on Mama's arrival.

Aunt Joy then took me and Chloe to Dr. Lanny Walker's vet clinic. Lanny was the former husband of Aunt Joy's niece Diane Honeycutt, also known as my second cousin. He was a well-known and caring vet in our community. I secretly hoped he might give me a little discount but was mostly just grateful that he would see little Chloe so quickly. He groomed, bathed, gave shots, and gave her love. Aunt Joy and I thanked him and let him know how much we appreciated him. When I reached to pay the bill he said "no charge". I knew that bill was about $250.00 and I was overwhelmed with gratitude. I was doing the right thing, Aunt Joy was doing the right thing, Neicy was doing the right thing, cousin Diane Taylor was doing the right thing and Dr. Lanny was doing the right thing. It was a love fest that was staggering! The kindness I was receiving on Mama's behalf engulfed me like a warm blanket. I could barely breathe, walk, talk, or do on that day. People all around me were walking with me and helping me through that harrowing and daunting day.

When I got back to Hospice that night my intent was to go home. I was exhausted. I told Mama that everything went great and I showed her pictures of her babies at or going to their forever home. She never knew Scooter had to go on to heaven. I showed her a picture of Scooter at the vet and Mama was elated that she was getting help. She smiled and softly said thank you and she never mentioned her babies again. The gift of peace in her heart knowing her babies were taken care of was evident. I couldn't leave the chair beside her. I was paralyzed, exhausted, devastated, and grateful. My feet wouldn't move but my daughters heart was full. I was mentally, physically, and emotionally spent. The hardest day of my life and the one that had the most love in it co-existed equally in my body. That day changed my life forever. What I witnessed went from tragedy and horror to bountiful and overflowing love, gratitude, and triumph. Who knew deep and powerful sorrow could coexist equally inside one's body at exactly the same time. I was beaming like a bone-weary beacon too!

All 4 dogs placed.
Thankful for Denise, Aunt Joy, Diane, Sandy Laughter Haulk, and Lanny Walker (they know what they did).
Morris ran off but came back.
I was glad to see him this morning.
He is going to Calli, my third cousin on Daddy's side.
Long ride home.
Thankful beyond words.
This might have been the toughest day of my life.
I had to turn in mama's car. She owed more than it was worth.
Aunt Joy followed me to the car lot.
I cleaned Mama's pitiful car out.
The odd pain that comes from tending to someone else's affairs can be crippling, especially when they are still alive.

I had to do what I had to do.
She only asked me about her car once.
She said "I guess they will come get my car."
I told her that her car was taken care of and she never mentioned it again.

Sandy Laughter (my distant cousin on Daddy's side) was a blessing and very helpful during that time. I love you Sandy.

Mama had taken various medicines for her mental illness most of her adult life. During her ten week stay at Hospice she took very little meds for what we all thought was a bipolar illness. I later learned after doing extensive research that Mama was never officially diagnosed as being bipolar. The recurrent and consistent diagnosis was major depression. At Hospice she was on a low dose of Ativan for anxiety. As she got sicker and her pain got worse I had the doctor increase her Ativan dosage. She was groggy and out of it for a day. She asked me to cut back on the dosage. We immediately did that. She said she didn't want to feel "out of it". I guess she knew her days left were few and she wanted to be present and lucid. That was just the opposite of Mama pre-Hospice. Pancreatic cancer is supposed to be painful, ugly, and swift. Her pain was well controlled. She had no nightmares, hallucinations, or none of the ugly symptoms that typically accompany that dreadful disease. To say we were grateful for that was an understatement. Mama was being reborn and experiencing a beautiful death simultaneously.

On Friday March 28, 2014 Allison Flynn of Hospice asked Mama if she would be interested in doing an interview for the Hospice House newsletter. She eagerly agreed. She was excited to share her experience with others. In the interview one of the last questions Allison asked her was "If you could sum up your experience at Hospice House of Rutherford County what would you say?" In a very slow, tired, deliberate, weak, and peaceful voice Mama said, "I wish everyone could feel the way they have made me feel." She wanted to encourage others to open their minds and hearts and choose Hospice and choose it sooner. She would have chosen Hospice much earlier if she would have known the real truth about it. The stigma stopped her from pursuing it sooner. It was her hope that her experience would help others find the care, love, hope, and restoration that she found through Hospice. It was the best decision Mama ever made. The cool thing about it was she and she alone finally took charge of her own life and fate. She decided to "Live Life To The Fullest" as the Hospice House of Rutherford County slogan states.

Chapter 43- Baby Girl and the JoyEful Noise

Joye had told me she didn't want to be there when Mama passed. I respected that. Aunt Joy and I stayed all week with Mama. However, when it was evident Mama's journey home was nearing, Joye came to be with her. Mama was waiting on something. She was holding on. We quickly came to realize Mama was waiting on her baby girl. Not me. Not a man. Not a savior. Not a miracle. She was waiting on her baby.

On April 2, 2017 Joye reflects on that. "How do you say good bye forever to the person that brought you into this world? No matter the relationship, it's very hard to say goodbye. This was different, I wasn't going to a funeral. I was literally getting to talk to her for one last time. She was hanging on and we knew the end was near. What would I say? How would I handle it? Would I break down or be strong for her? I did just that. Just like the whole journey of her illness (well for my whole life really) it wasn't about me it was about her!"

Joye continued "That night was harder than her passing. I let her talk, as her voice got weaker, I took over the conversation. I made her laugh as I did every day when she went to hospice. I told her, "Mom when you see the Angels don't hesitate, don't look back for me and Robbie. We will be ok. Take the Lord's hand and flyaway. She said "I'm proud of you!" Then she started repeating whatever I said and she went silent. She wouldn't hang up the phone because she was holding her "baby girl". Not one day do I miss the woman who I knew my whole life, the woman who didn't take care of me, who let me go and find someone else to do her job! But not one day goes by that I don't think about the woman she became when she entered hospice and found peace in her life she never experienced. I miss that woman!"

They had come to peace in their relationship. Mama was forgiven and therefore set free. Her chains were gone. Her shackles were released and her mind untangled!

Aunt Joy, Little Joye, and myself were taking turns sitting up with Mama. We were adamant she would never be alone again nor would she cross the river alone. I was adamant that I wouldn't miss her last breath. I couldn't. It was a fact that I would witness my Mama's last breath as surely as she witnessed my first breath.

Mama's feet had started mottling. That happens when blood settles and leaves spots on the skin. That's one of the signs of physical death. Her breathing changed a little but nothing dramatic and for a day or two her eyes were open. They were cloudy and she appeared to be looking into the distance at something or someone. We knew it was angels. She had told us a while back that women had been coming into her room. We steadfastly knew it was angels. I was sitting beside Mama and the "Joy's" were laying on the pull out bed resting. We had been sitting vigilant and taking turns all night. I could tell Mama's breathing had changed a little more and I could feel her spirit in the air. She wasn't afraid of death instead she embraced it gracefully. She was as ready to go as an early spring flower pushing at the ground to bloom. I knew the time was upon us. I felt it in my blood, bones, and on my skin. I wasn't taking my eyes off Mama so I texted the Joy's and told them to come over that it was time.

They came and we all three stood by her bedside. Aunt Joy was at her feet and Little Joye and I were on each side of her. We held hands. She took a small breath and exhaled softly, quietly, perfectly, and beautifully closed her eyes and floated into the sunny Carolina spring morning. We were giddy and drunk with miracle dust and God's favor like manna. There was no drama. We felt weightless in her presence as if we were astronauts floating in space and time. We could feel the angels on our skin. It was a divine gift from the heavens. We had literally been a part of a real miracle. The preyed on became the prayed with. The victim became a victor and the broken had become a beacon.

It was around 7:00 am. The three of us were just standing there taking it all in. There was an amazing and inexplicable joy that took over the room. Her face was sweet and loving and so full of peace that there was zero sorrow! Can I get an Amen! There was emphatically no sorrow in that room. The angels came and took her as surely as the sun rose that morning. She looked like a glorious angel. She got her freedom and most of all the peace that she had been looking for all her life. Her girls had forgiven her and she had finally forgiven herself. She became free like the bird she had explained to me about earlier. I finally called Mama's nurse Ashley and she came down and called Mama's time of death at 0716. The Joy's and me left the room for a few minutes while Ashley did all the legal things that were supposed to occur. Ashley came to me and told me the Chase High School student CNA's were doing their internship and would it be all right if they helped. That is the school that our entire family went to and some were still going to. We agreed to allow that to happen. We knew without a doubt Mama would endorse it. When they were through Ashley called us back in the room. Mama had crossed the river but her body was still with us. They had pulled her hair up off of her neck and put a little makeup on her. Mama would have been pleased. She loved to look pretty and doll up a bit. My friend John Little and his bride had sent Mama a dozen long stemmed roses a few days earlier. Ashley got one of the roses and placed it in Mama's hands. They fixed her purple blanket the way she liked it. Mama looked like a 50's movie star! She was elegant. Her neck looked long and slim in a beautiful and striking way. She had grown into the person she was born to be. The sorrow, pain, and regret was gone from her face. We were elated! Mama was glory bound. The Joy's and I were drunk with gratitude and the experience. For the first time in my life I was thankful to be her spittin' image. It was a dream come true for two little girls that longed for their Mama and her happiness. We were becoming beacons too and now I want to see what my Mama saw.

After Mama crossed the river I sat in her room alone for a few minutes. The journey had been exhausting and felt like one long day. I was sitting on the couch and the door to her room was open. I looked down at the bottom of the door and there were three perfect hearts naturally made in the grain of the wood. I took multiple photos of those hearts and they eventually turned into artwork. It was another blessing in the pain. Thank you Mama.

"And the angels came and they changed her name from the wrong to the righteous".

Section Five: The Angels

Chaplain Cecelia Beck

Mama's Chaplain at Hospice House of Rutherford County, NC.

Your mother was admitted to Hospice House on 1/23/14 and I met her on 1/24/14. She was very lethargic, appeared to be very depressed and was miserable from constant itching. Despite all that, she was very gracious and accepting of my visit. When I offered to visit again soon, she readily accepted and gave me a very weak smile. Within 3 days her countenance had changed. She was in much better spirits and that continued to improve day by day. She went from someone who clearly did not care if she lived or died and appeared "hopeless" to someone who clearly had hope. She smiled and enjoyed and welcomed everyone who interacted with her.

I'm sorry I don't remember the last conversation but all conversations in her final days were filled with her expressions of gratitude and love. As I have shared before, I saw that God had indeed "restored the years that the locusts had eaten." She was at peace with herself and was accepting of her impending death and looking forward to freedom from the pain of this world. Despite obvious disease progression and pain, she never complained after her outlook changed. She graciously accepted whatever changes took place in her functioning and discomfort.

I have never witnessed such a change from hopelessness and depression to deep peace, tranquility, gratitude, and underlying joy.

Joel 2:25 I will repay you for the years the locusts have eaten.

Danielle Smart Williams

Mama's Social Worker at Hospice House of Rutherford County, NC.

My first impression of her was that she looked afraid. I don't know if she was but she definitely looked afraid. By the next week I got to see a different side of her. She looked much more at peace and no longer afraid. It is not uncommon for any nursing home to turn down someone with mental illness. Before any patient can go to a facility they have to receive a PASSR #. I have to go online to a state website and answer information on a person's mental health history, provide a medicine list, report any psychiatric hospitalization, any behaviors, etc. I am not positive but I think I remember she had made a suicidal statement while in the hospital. I am not 100% sure on that. Anyway with a PASSR # you can get level A or B. She would probably have had a B. A lot of facilities don't want to take patients with a B level PASSR. She is definitely a patient I will never forget. I was and still am thankful that it worked out for her to stay with us. That is when she began to look at peace. We all loved her very much.

Lisa Humphries Tolleson

One of Mama's special CNA's at Hospice House of Rutherford County, NC.

When I first met her she did not say much. Every time I went into her room after that I would just joke and cut up with her. Well, one day I went in to give her a bath and we got to talking about things we used to do and come to find out we knew a lot of the same people. We started talking about what they were doing now. I got to where I couldn't wait to go in there and talk to her and check to see how she was doing each day. There were days when she did not feel like talking but she would still come back with something humorous. She never complained about nothing. I remember you (Robbie) getting her those angel's and different charms to give to us. To this day I still have my angel charm. I miss our talks and I won't ever forget her because she had an everlasting inspirational effect on me.

Reverend Debbie Potter

Mama's niece via Daddy's sister and spiritual warrior

Ms. Barbara came into my life quickly after a lifetime of absence, placed there by the hand of God during a time of grief and loss of the only love she ever knew, my precious uncle. Ms. Barbara told me a story that day, she asked about my mom and remarked that in their younger days, how my mom was slender and Ms. Barbara was heavy and now those roles were reversed, how she had felt less than and never quite good enough for the family or my uncle. She was brutally honest. My memories as a young girl were those of a smiling beautiful woman …. The eyes of a child see kindness and beauty when it is present. I was not aware of all the turmoil that had existed in her life during those years but I sensed a person with a need. It was only a very short time until her diagnosis. When I learned of her illness I felt so compelled to see her and I was so honored when she said she would love for me to come to Hospice. When I saw her, I knew the Lord had ordained this time …. A TIME FOR PEACE. She took to my sweet husband, Jackie, and her eyes would light up when he came into the room. An instant love had been formed that only the Lord could have placed there and with that love came trust, with trust … hope, with hope …. Peace. Finally… peace. We began to visit and the love and trust grew.

My focus is one particular day that the Lord impressed me to go to her and read the bible to her. It was a quiet day …. Just she and I … and the Word of God. The scripture was Psalm 107:23-30.

They that go down to the sea in ships, that do business in great waters; These see the works of the LORD, and his wonders in the deep. For he commandeth, and raiseth the stormy wind, which lifteth up the waves thereof. They mount up to the heaven, they go down again to the depths: their soul is melted because of trouble. They reel to and fro, and stagger like a drunken man, and are at their wits' end. Then they cry unto the LORD in their trouble, and he bringeth them out of their distresses. He maketh the storm a calm, so that the waves thereof are still. Then are they glad because they be quiet; so he bringeth them unto their desired haven.

She loved the sea … the Lord loved her but she didn't know that he loved HER … that He loved her with an everlasting love ….

I saw the realization in her eyes that she saw herself in that scripture and acknowledged where her help would come from …. Calling on the Lord …. "then they are glad because they be quiet so he bringeth them unto their desired haven" ….. for Ms. Barbara … it was the haven of the peace of God that passeth all understandings.

Words of regret, words of forgiveness and words of hope were spoken that day. But the unspoken words … the ones that the spirit of the Lord spoke that day were the difference. Man looks on the appearance but the Lord looks on the heart. What a beautiful heart he saw that day … a heart that desired to be with him and know fully His peace. The spirit moved that day between me and Ms. Barbara and it changed us both … she made a commitment to her Savior and I made a commitment to her … a commitment that will take a lifetime but I fully intend to keep.

Ms. Barbara knew that her time was short and that peace had been found. In that quiet place, she was thinking of the two people she loved most, the two people that she had brought the most joy and likely the most pain, the two that stood by her in her darkest moments and in her final peaceful days, the two that she wanted to know how very much they meant to her. Her final talk with me in our last conversation alone was a confidential request, to honor those two … Robbie and Joye … her heart. Ms. Barbara asked that I arrange to have the song "The Wind Beneath My Wings" sung at her funeral to leave that knowledge with her precious daughters … that she could not have done life without them.

Ms. Barbara's final days are a testimony of the peace of God that I can now share with others in like need. The Lord surely blessed me that day ….

Reverend Jackie Potter

Mama's example of a gentleman

When I first met Barbara, unfortunately for me she was already in the throes of passing from this life. My first thought was what can I say about what I'm seeing... I knew that this small, frail little woman was in a constant state of unknown and yet there was a way that she looked at me that made me know that she wanted something from me. It wasn't long before someone whispered in my ear to pray that she would have peace... So I did. Not long after that another request became an object of my prayers so I asked my wife Deborah to help me pray about that. She did. We felt compelled after praying to tell Barbara that we would not leave her alone. We didn't. Loneliness and fear are two of the most debilitating conditions of the soul that one might encounter. There was a constant statement from the lips of Jesus that said "Fear Not" and "Peace Be Unto You".

I felt compelled after praying to tell Barbara that we would not leave her alone. We didn't. Loneliness and fear are two of the most debilitating conditions of the soul that one might encounter. There was a constant statement from the lips of Jesus that said "Fear Not" and "Peace Be Unto You". If it was His desire then it should be ours. If we are truly the children of The Most High God we should be obedient unto Him.

Loneliness and fear are two of the most debilitating conditions of the soul that one might encounter. There was a constant statement from the lips of Jesus that said "Fear Not" and "Peace Be Unto You". If it was His desire then it should be ours. If we are truly the children of The Most High God we should be obedient unto Him.

Matthew 10:12-13

12 And when ye come into a house, salute it.

13 And if the house be worthy, let your peace come upon it: but if it be not worthy, let your peace return to you. I can say that every time we visited Barbara, the peace of God grew stronger every time and Barbara became more content and confident that she was not alone.

It's a wonderful feeling to know that a simple visit with one who is suffering and fearful can make such a difference in their life. Even greater is the assurance that we have fulfilled our Lord's commission. I will always cherish the opportunity to minister to Barbara with my wife and to know that in some small way we gained her trust and love. Above all, we will cherish the hope of seeing her again when we enter the gates of heaven where she waits.

Choices

Does my Mama have choices
Does she hear voices
Is she lazy or crazy
Does she have the mental health shuffle
Does she struggle
Why can't she get off the couch
She's not a slouch
Of that I can vouch
Why is she not treated with the same dignity and respect as medical patients
I'm losing my patience
With the discrimination about mental health
When the medical field has the wealth
Putting her on a shelf
On a shelf that no one can heal
How low does that make her feel
And how can she deal
When it kills
Her spirit and her drive
And she is simply trying to survive and stay alive
Much less thrive
I ask you does my Mama have choices
The bad decisions
The pain
The bad decisions and shame
Is she to blame
Like when she is locked up
And the system is messed up
And when she leaves and all she takes with her is a bookmark she made in craft class
Now I ask you does my Mama have choices
I mean what is bipolar
Bi means 2 and polar means opposite sides
She goes from high to low
And low to high
Feel the sky
Then pick the wrong guy

Then lie and cry
It is chemical
It is her brain like sunshine and rain
All mixed up like oh lord the devil is beating his wife
And I ask you if my Mama had choices
I do
I choose to tell y'all this here today
And hopefully it will stay
With you and me
And we are all the same in the eyes of the great creator
And I tell you he made her perfect just the way she was
And today she stands among the angels
And I ask you does my Mama have choices
Damn straight
She walked through the gate
Where there is no hate and lows
Only highs
She's in the sky with Betty Jean
And she has seen
The power and the glory of her own story
And what love can do
And treating someone with dignity and respect
And the pure love of the all mighty
She rolled through the doors of the hospice church
And the visitors flocked to witness the BROKEN BECOME A BEACON
And the preyed on became the prayed with
And the victim became a victor
She had dreams with angels in them
There were angels with names like Cecilia, Courtney, Ashley and Lincoln, Karen and Chrissy, Judy
and Linda, Danielle, Lisa, Tracy, Fran, Sherry, Brooke, Phoebe, Denita, Peggy, Elisha, and Shica.
And now I tell you my mama had choices
And she chose the supreme redeemer's grace
And ran the race
To see his face
And it all fell into place
She is free
She is a seagull
And now she sees her girls

Every second of every minute of every earthly hour
She has the ultimate peace that she so desperately sought and bought with her soul
She is picking up seashells
She has sand between her toes
And she knows the Big Joye and the Little Joye of all things perfect
And when the winds from the Gail's blew
And she knew
She had become new
And I tell you my Mama had choices
She is as clearly at Myrtle Beach
And within reach as a smoking hot Ocean Boulevard Drive
She is as alive as Peaches Corner in July
And she flies over the Gay Dolphin and 2nd Avenue pier
And it is as clear as a Memorial week-end at The Pavilion
But it don't end here
Let me be clear
When she came through these doors
She was running from the repo man
The reaper
And death
And the taste of metal from chemo on her breath
And she could not rest
She said Rob I'm done
And she chose the sun
Dr. H. said she might not make it through the week
She was weak
And seemed meek and mild
And I tell you my mama had choices
She chose to accept the crown
And dismiss the frown
She touched the hands that were held out to her
And the last 64 years became a blur
And the way things were
Melted like cornbread in the buttermilk that she was about to drink
The miracle and spirits
I know we could both hear it
It is real
And it made her feel

Like a lost lamb that had found its way
They let us know that if you need anything
Quickly turned into I love you's
And her blues turned her frown upside down
And her heart beat so loud
That she pushed through the dirt
Like a crocus after a frigid winter
The care was there
But the pure love of the all hands that graced her Lilac/Willow suite
And kissed her sweet face
And spent their own precious time just to show they care
And share a look or a memory
And she chose to accept this divine gift of their calling
And she began falling in love with life
And she did not want to leave
But believe that when her God whispered through the clouds
It is time to take my hand
And listen to the angel band
And come on gal let's go see your mama
All the trauma and drama ceased to be
And now we see
What her choices were when it really mattered
Her final wish came to fruition
And she was wishing
And her two greatest accomplishments
Each had one of her hands as she floated like a vapor into the spring morning
Ronda Patton saved my life she said…………….

Chapter 44- No Depression in Heaven

On Saturday April 12, 2014 we cleaned Mama's house out from end to end. It was true. Mama's belongings were gone. Her clothes, Christmas presents, jewelry, and all of her shoes. Everything that she owned that was salvageable and worth money was gone. I knew what happened but it was a battle not worth fighting. I had her things that really mattered. They were not things at all. I had her heart. Things were different. Life was different. Joye was different. I was different. That was a challenging day for me but made easier with the support and help of my family. It took all day but my loves kept the mood light and funny. We made a sad situation a joyful day. Everywhere I turned throughout this journey there were women standing beside me and helping me EVERY SINGLE STEP!

Aunt Patsy asked me if I had come across a strawberry Christmas ornament while cleaning out Mama's things. I told her that we did not. That is when she told me the story of the strawberry ornament and its significance in their relationship. She and Mama would sometimes whisper to each other when Aunt Patsy visited Mama at Hospice. They would giggle and laugh and were sometimes talking about the ornament and whose turn it was to have it.

Mama's celebration was held on April 13, 2014. We wanted to have it on the Hospice House grounds so we rented the Carolina's Conference Center which is part of Hospice House of Rutherford County. Not only was it an unbelievably beautiful place, the money we paid went right back into the Hospice funds. It is the best kept secret in Rutherford County, NC! That was exactly what Mama would have wished for. The room was huge and it had a stage, grand fireplace, and gorgeous sitting area. We served sweet tea and we did not have a book to sign in. Instead we had optional note cards for people to share a memory of Mama. Pictures of Mama and our family were mounted on easels amongst flowers, sand, seashells, and some of Mama's favorite things including her Tar Heel hat. Aunt Joy had bought an enormous vase of flowers just for Mama's special day. We had 200 chairs set up for guests and we rented a sound guy. It turned out that the sound guy was the son of one of Mawmaw's best friends. Small town blessings rock! We used purple sashes and sectioned off some seats for our family and for the Hospice House workers that took care of Mama. They were now a part of our family. My sister and I wore all black clothes with beautiful purple scarves to honor Mama. Aunt Joy and Aunt Gail also wore black and purple. It was a unique and unorthodox celebration.

Two Hospice House volunteer angels kicked things off by singing a very country medley of Precious Lord and various southern hymns. Mama wanted the Reverend's Jackie and Debbie Potter to be involved. Debbie was the master of ceremonies and Jackie and his daughter Christy sang No Depression In Heaven for Mama. Joye and I spoke and Eric Wilson sang and played Free/Into The Mystic and Amazing Grace/My Chains Are Gone.

We recognized and thanked the Hospice workers. I took my purple scarf off and put it around Ronda Patton's neck and thanked her. That is exactly what Mama would have wanted me to do. We showed a video of Mama's girls and then a Hospice video to thank them publicly.

We were getting up to head outside for the releasing of the doves when Debbie told us to sit back down. She said that Mama had asked her to surprise me and Joye and have Christy Potter (Jackie's daughter) sing Wind Beneath My Wings for her two greatest assets. We were blown away! Thank you Mama. Thank you for that. Joye and me were so blessed.

We didn't get Mama a headstone or burial plot. Instead we bought an "In Loving Memory of Barbara Robbins" brick that was placed on the walkway at the entrance to Hospice House. Mama was immortalized on the grounds of the place that saved her life, Hospice House of Rutherford County, NC. The proceeds from purchasing the brick went right back into our beloved Hospice House.

Chapter 45- Finally Free and Forever at the Beach

June 1, 2014 Joye and me met at the 2nd Ave Pier at Mama's favorite place, Myrtle Beach, SC. I had some of Mama's ashes in a sand bucket along with some of her seashells she had collected over the years. Little Joye and I grabbed hands full of ashes and tossed them up into the wind. There she went, just like she wanted. She told me she wanted freedom like a bird. We walked out into the water and scattered her more wildly and with abandon. Me and Joye were having a blast. We were laughing and celebrating Mama exactly how she wanted us to. We then took some of her ashes and mixed them in with some sand. We built a sandcastle and wrote her a note in the sand. Her two greatest assets set her free! Oh what a happy Mama spirit she was that day. Mama was dancing eternally in the sand and on the waves and her two greatest assets were dancing around her.

Update

Me and Joye have grown closer just like Mama wanted. We help each other in our new endeavors. I have a project called "The Dark Corner Project". My project helps educate people on mentalillness, domestic violence, and the real truth about hospice. I help feral cats and find homes for dogs in neglectful situations. I am also a certified volunteer at the local Hospice House. I educate and witness to families and visits patients.

Joye helps feral cats by feeding them, ensuring they are spay/neutered and secures warm shelters for them in the cold weather. She finds homes for kittens that were born to feral cats. Her project is called "The Remington Project" and can be found on Facebook. There is a link to my project on Joye's page and a link to Joye's project on my page. Me and Joye are both doing our little part to honor our parents and to make the world a better place. We both got the very best of both of our parents.

"The Aunts" Big Joy and Aunt Gail have lived up to their end of the promise they made with Mama. They promised to look after us and they have. They have remained an active force in our lives. I love those two Honeycutt women with everything inside of me. They represent tradition, family, and blood. They love Little Joye and me unconditionally. Aunt Joy is a volunteer at Hospice House of Rutherford County. Once a week she greets visitors, shows them where to go, and sometimes gives her testimony about the miracle that happened there. She visits Mama's brick every week.

Each Christmas since Mama passed I have hunted and found Aunt Patsy a special strawberry Christmas ornament. I look forward to wrapping it up all pretty and shipping it to her. She and I now have a tradition that I plan to keep for the rest of her life. Aunt Patsy has stayed in touch with me and always asks about Joye. She is a special and direct link to Mama. It makes my heart swell knowing she is in my life and loves me.

About the Author

Robbie Taylor was born and raised in the foothills of North Carolina. She loves sports, photography, reading, writing, and volunteering at Hospice. This is her first book and she hopes to shed light on other children like her and her sister, mental illness, domestic violence, the real truth about Hospice, and share hope when you are certain there is none. Love always wins and where there is breath there is hope. Her sister Joye Taylor was pivotal in making this project successful and helping the book come to fruition.

You can find more information at www.brokentobeacon.com.

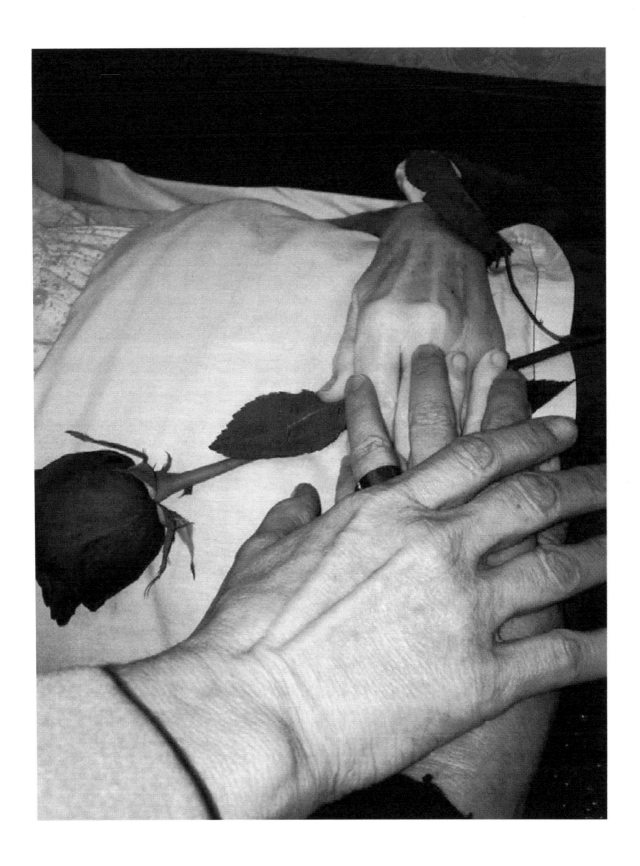